T0193262

Ignite
PRAISE

MONIQUE LETTIRE

WESTBOW
PRESS®
A DIVISION OF THOMAS NELSON
& ZONDERVAN

Copyright © 2022 Monique Lettire.

All rights reserved. No part of this book may be used or reproduced by any means, graphic, electronic, or mechanical, including photocopying, recording, taping or by any information storage retrieval system without the written permission of the author except in the case of brief quotations embodied in critical articles and reviews.

WestBow Press books may be ordered through booksellers or by contacting:

WestBow Press
A Division of Thomas Nelson & Zondervan
1663 Liberty Drive
Bloomington, IN 47403
www.westbowpress.com
844-714-3454

Because of the dynamic nature of the Internet, any web addresses or links contained in this book may have changed since publication and may no longer be valid. The views expressed in this work are solely those of the author and do not necessarily reflect the views of the publisher, and the publisher hereby disclaims any responsibility for them.

Any people depicted in stock imagery provided by Getty Images are models, and such images are being used for illustrative purposes only. Certain stock imagery © Getty Images.

Scripture quotations taken from the (NASB®) New American Standard Bible®, Copyright © 1960, 1971, 1977, 1995, 2020 by The Lockman Foundation. Used by permission. All rights reserved. www.lockman.org

Scripture taken from the New King James Version® Copyright © 1982 by Thomas Nelson. Used by permission. All rights reserved.

Scripture quotations marked (NLT) are taken from the Holy Bible, New Living Translation, copyright ©1996, 2004, 2015 by Tyndale House Foundation. Used by permission of Tyndale House Publishers, a Division of Tyndale House Ministries, Carol Stream, Illinois 60188. All rights reserved.

Scripture quotations taken from The Holy Bible, New International Version® NIV® Copyright © 1973 1978 1984 2011 by Biblica, Inc. TM. Used by permission. All rights reserved worldwide.

ISBN: 978-1-6642-7529-4 (sc)
ISBN: 978-1-6642-7530-0 (hc)
ISBN: 978-1-6642-7565-2 (e)

Library of Congress Control Number: 2022915132

Print information available on the last page.

WestBow Press rev. date: 10/11/2022

Work of Art

Father, you care about me
More than the birds of the air.
I am your daughter.
I need only to be still,
For you are here in my midst.
I don't need to be scared;
I don't have to fear because I am your dear one.
For you say, in your word, I am chosen, So yes
Lord, I will do your will.
For your word says to be still and know that you're God.
For so long, I tried to do your job.
The world tried to rob my heart,
But you had a plan for me, from the start.
God, you set me apart.
I am your poema, your beautiful work of art!
You have cleansed me and redeemed me.
You are the God who sees me.
You're lifting my head;
You want me to lean on you instead.
This world has nothing to offer, for this daughter.
You have put a hunger, for purity, in me.
Holy Spirit is the security within me;
He is making me anew.
This new desire, of wholehearted devotion, is being birthed.
Now I'm beginning to see my worth.
This is what you have wanted from me, since my birth,
For you to know me
And I know you,
Intimately
And legitimately.
I will watch, as you set me free,
In you.

Genesis 16:13 "She gave this name to the Lord who spoke to her: 'You are the God who sees me,' for she said, 'I have now seen the One who sees me.'" —NIV Did you know that we are His poema, His work of art!

Ephesians 2:10 "For we are His *workmanship, created in Christ Jesus for good works, which God prepared beforehand that we should walk in them." —ESV Workmanship is the Hebrew word poema, which means to make a poem or poetry.

We are a design, produced by the greatest artisan.
Poema emphasizes God as the master designer. The whole universe is His creation, and the redeemed believers are His new creation. Amen.

Blossom

Blossom my flower, Look at your beautiful buds,
Each one, with its own story.
I won't let anyone pluck them away.
I am so proud of you.
I can breathe you in forever.
I have set my seal on you.
You're mine.
I watch over you daily, As long as the sun shines
And during your sweet sleep.
I am your rock,
Your refuge,
Your hiding place.
In the shelter of me,
Demons flee.
I have called you out.
Arise my beautiful one,
Go show others this marvelous love,
This love I have extended to you.
Arise, Arise!

Be the example,
I have poured out my fragrance all over you.
Your eyes are burning, with my fiery love.
I have given you my heart,
This heart full of compassion for my children.
The world is mine, And I love it.
The people are mine, And I long for them.
Though most of them may not know me,
Though they may reject me, I know them.
They were with me, before the foundations of the earth.
I have loved them, with an everlasting love.
The very hairs on their head, I know.

I have written their stories.
Oh, if they only knew their powerful identity in me!
The inheritance I so willingly would give them!
Go, get my brides for me,
Bring all the prodigals home.
I long to give them life;
I long to pour out my grace all over them.
How I yearn for my creation!
My people made in my very image!
Oh, my heart!
Let's get them together.
I'll hold your hand and teach you;
I'll instruct you, with patience and love.
I have placed the sword of the spirit in your hands.
Your prayers have created it.
Your sweet intercession,
The fruit of your lips.
Speaking life, declaring healing,
Go, the victory is ours.
My army of angels surrounds you,
Ministering strength to you.

Hell will not prevail against you.
See, I am doing a new thing.
The religious chains, I will break off of my people.
My spirit will be poured upon all flesh.
Then they will all know me.
Freedom, I will set all of them free!
I, yes, I, the Lord, am doing this.

Psalm 91:1 "He that dwelleth in the secret place of the most
High shall abide under the shadow of the Almighty" —KJV

Isaiah 43:19 "See, I am doing a new thing! Now it springs up; do you not perceive it? I am making a way in the wilderness and streams in the wasteland." —NIV

Galatians 5:1 "It is for freedom that Christ has set us free." —NIV

Psalm 32:8 "I will instruct you and teach you in the way you should go; I will counsel you with my loving eye on you." —NIV

Acts 2:17 "In the last days," God says, "I will pour out my Spirit upon all people. Your sons and daughters will prophesy. Your young men will see visions, and your old men will dream dreams." —NLT

Salvation

I got saved when I was twenty-one.
I told the Lord I'm living for Him and not no one.
This is my calling.
I've spent too many days stalling.
When He saved me that fire burned in and out and through.
He told me that I was brand new.
I'm living, to give Him glory.
This is my story.
Was addicted, to alcohol and pills,
Used to get high from the thrills.
Emotionally and sexually abused,
I was so used.
Was with a man that had no respect for my body;

His behavior was always shoddy.
Have daddy issues, so I had to develop this hobby,
To write to escape from all the pain.
But thank God, for the lamb that was slain.
Listen to me; His death was not in vain.
The enemy was wrapped around me, like a chain.
I was so ignorant, like Cain.
But the Lord came into my life and drained away all of me that was lame.
I just want to live this life and give Him full fame.
The Lord took me and gave me a new name.
I believed Him.
Jesus saves any and every one;
He's my number one.
You think you got it bad?
I thought I did too, then I looked at Paul, and I knew
That, if the Lord saved him, He also gave me His all too.

Don't let people talk down on you.
If you got a calling, a destiny, you better walk out on it.
Don't waste your God given talents, it's a gift.
I'm here, to give your heart a lift,
To show you that you're not alone.
The Lord wants to make your heart His home,
So you can, one day, be in the presence of His throne!
I use to look in the mirror and think my insides were so ugly.
Thought those around me were my friends, but really, I had nobody.
I was on the search for something real, Found my community in church.
That's where I found true love and my family.
I've had a lot of sleepless nights,
Wasteful fights, with God, in prayer.
So many times, I thought I was talking to the air.
But He showed me He is there.
He's always cared,
And I'm no longer scared.
He saved me from Hell.
I used to dwell in the darkness.
But God renewed all of me and made me well.
I'm a walking testimony, of His goodness.
I just gotta do it;
I gotta teach people about Jesus.
Don't live for this world.
These fake things, they'll make your spirit hurl.
I used to think my comfort was in the finer things, money and blings.
But when we leave this Earth, we won't bring any of those things,
Just the love that we left behind.
And when we die,

God is going to rewind
All that we did.
So live your life full of faith, like a kid.
Kids don't question His faithfulness.
Remember when you were young and your parents taught you that God is real?
Then, when we get older, the weight of the world feels heavier on our shoulders,
And we cross over to the desires of sin.
By choosing, with our free will, to be blind to God, we allow the enemy to secretly win.
Don't listen to those demon liars that try to get in.
We wrestle not against flesh and blood.
God says it in the Bible, just look,
None of us are off the hook.
We need to partner with His spirit,
So we can conquer the gates of Hell and the world can hear it.
He's seeking after full revival,
But we gotta get thru these trials.
It can sometimes feel like it can go on for miles.
He says, "Are you in, no matter the cost?"
"Are you willing to lay down your life for the lost?"
Because He did.
And we are meant to be more like Him.
We can only be transformed by letting His spirit dwell within.
So let Him in,
And let Him win.

Luke 19:10 "For the Son of Man came to seek and save those who are lost." —NLT Matthew 18:2–4 "He called a

little child to him, and placed the child among them. And he said:

'Truly I tell you, unless you change and become like little children, you will never enter the kingdom of heaven.'"
—NIV

Colossians 1:13 "For He rescued us from the domain of darkness, and transferred us to the kingdom of His beloved Son, in whom we have redemption, the forgiveness of sins."
—NASB 1995

Excommunicated

A poem written after being betrayed by those in the church.
I'm broken.
My heart has been abused
And misused
There's a stain on the pain
That has hit my heart in vain.
I can't attain anything real in this world.
Hear me complain, Lord;
I can't contain
This sorrow.
Laying in bed, thinking of everything that was said.
I wish you could get into my head
And take away this dread.
Don't you see how dead my feelings are?
It might take a while to get over.
Be careful who you trust,
Who you give your heart to,
Cause, in the end, they might only regard you as dust.
Now I must strategize
On ways to move on and stay strong
Cause some people will never apologize
They want to live in their lies
They forget the truth and how to apply indeed
On how to love their neighbors as themselves
I gave my heart away
I've shown you how I'd be there all the time
You shoved me out the door
God, I can't do this anymore!
Jesus, help me!
You will know people by their fruit
When you look closely at their lives

Cause when certain people are not behind closed doors,
they try to hypnotize
Those around them, the sheep to believe how they
might be
But on the inside, its deception
Don't be fooled by how people try to change your
perception.

I hope they all come to the light
And you Lord shine bright to their sight
And help them to make you their delight
In all their ways
For your name's sake
Give them revelation to be the people that you created
them to be
And not who they've been
And Lord, help me to let go
To forgive and to find peace within.

Psalm 41:9 "Even my close friend, someone I trusted, one
who shared my bread, has turned against me" —NIV

"But I tell you, love your enemies and pray for those who
persecute you, that you may be children of your Father in
heaven." Matthew 5:44-45 —NIV

"But Jesus would not entrust himself to them, for he knew
all people. He did not need any testimony about mankind,
for he knew what was in each person" John 2:24 —NIV

Hurt

A poem written after being heartbroken by a mother figure that was in my life.
Sometimes a mother figure will hurt you
You open your heart to someone, and they break it
I shared deep things with you
Now you treat me like a stranger
Endangered my faith you did
And act like our relationship never existed
I came to this place for healing
Now you want space and boundaries
You broke my heart
Those closest to you can crush your spirit
She cried on me as I wept
Then hate crept in and changed her mind
How could you be so cold?
What happened in your old age?
I can't just turn the page and move on.
This is a phase of my life where I'm trying to be strong
But you were wrong
Were you always this way, Fair one?
You caused my heart to have a nasty scar
Though you broke me
I'll fight to the end
I'll walk through the storm
I want to say thank you
Thank you for showing me what I never want to do to someone else
If a young girl ever looks up to me, I'll never kill her the way you killed me
What did I do?
What did I do?
To make you shatter me anyway?

Why take someone under your wing just to sting their
emotions?
Forgiving you feels so hard
I want justice for what you did to me
Clenching my fists, asking God to calm the anger inside
I don't want unforgiveness to reside
But how could you not swallow up your pride?
Do you want to die without ever making things right?
Does love even exist inside of you?
I truly pray you will open up your eyes
Go and read Matthew 18:6
Call me and apologize
But no
You did this to many others too
How can you not discern you have a problem?
One day you'll learn
Lord God, why is this leader so unwilling?
Please, God, do something
Make things right
Lord, I know you're there
Hear me as I cast my care
Listen
Please help me to forgive until I feel it
Cause God, I still care And I always will.

Matthew 18:6 "If anyone causes one of these little ones—
those who believe in me—to stumble, it would be better
for them to have a large millstone hung around their neck
and to be drowned in the depths of the sea." —NIV

Reader, God cares about you. He cares about church
hurt and is not okay with whatever abuse you may have

experienced from a Christian leader. You're not alone in your pain. God will judge them. I want to encourage you and let you know it's okay to feel what you feel. Learn to give it to God and seek the help that you need, even from a trusted counselor if need be.

Dear Family

I'm thinking of what to say it's hard to formulate the
words
How to express my care for you?
How to make you aware of the truth that I allude to?
I've spoken about Him before
And I will again once more
Dear family, let me tell you what the gospel message is
Christ defeated death so you could live
Through the Death of Jesus on the cross, He takes away
your sin
Former sins are counted as a loss, as you become crucified
with Him
Through His resurrection, death is defeated
By His Ascension, powers of darkness depleted
Devils' hold on the world became broken
As Jesus showed Himself and has spoken
This is good news
Because no longer will you have to be under the ruse of
the world
Jesus conquered death, sin, and the devil for you
The enemy doesn't hold a grip
Because Christ the savior took a whip
With a metal led tip
39 times He was scourged for your crimes
This was the Fathers plan
I pray you read and understand
What this man suffered at his enemy's hand
God came to the earth in the form of a human
So you could know your worth
And may experience a new birth
When He was mocked and tortured
Blindfolded and spit on

He allowed Himself to be abused by the people that He created
He patiently endured and waited
For the joy set before Him, He drank the cup of suffering
Because He knew His blood would provide a covering
May your lips make professions of Him
As you call out for His name, watch Him take away your shame
This God who can heal the lame wants to draw you in
Renounce your sins
Stop choosing your own paths
Why be a child of wrath?
God gives you free will
He will not force His hand on you
If it is your own course that you choose to take
Just know that your creator feels remorse
When you reject His son
And what He's done
Dear family,
No, not being "just a good person" counts
It doesn't even amount to how you will inherit eternal life
Because none of us are good
Only by grace through faith can you be genuinely saved
Listen, Dear Ones,
Doing what "feels good" will lead to death and destruction
Until one day, you wake up in the devil's dungeon
By then, it will be too late
Weeping and gnashing of teeth will be your fate
But there is a God in heaven who is real
The truth of Him I will no longer conceal
Even the demons hear of His name and shiver
He has a river that never runs dry
We will one day all give an account to Him
Jesus said He is the only way

Turn your hearts to Him today
Change your minds
Please, search yourselves and recognize your need for the
savior of the world.
Oh, Dear Family
It's a beautiful exchange
He is not a distant God
Once you believe in your heart and confess His Lordship,
you become His child.
It gets personal as you become eternal through Him
It's not just about sitting in a church pew
Or saying prayers that make you feel good too
Instead the Father wants you to have a heart transition
As you accept Jesus' blood for the remission of your sins
It's your insides that God wants to revive
A new fire, a new passion come alive
A purpose renewed as God makes you new
Deep down inside, you know I am right So why are you
fighting the one true light?
Why spite the maker?
It's all of Him or nothing
Cant self justify
Mixing your own rights with His word is a lie
His word is infallible
It shall never pass, its valuable
The Lord holds true wisdom
Lean on Him with your life's decision
Call on the name of Jesus
The only name that can save
The only name that can deliver you from the power of
the grave.

1 Timothy 2: "who wants all people to be saved and to come to a knowledge of the truth. For there is one God and one mediator between God and mankind, the man Christ Jesus, who gave himself as a ransom for all people." —NIV

John 14:6 Jesus said to him, "I am the way, and the truth, and the life. No one comes to the Father except through me. —ESV

John 1:12 "But to all who believed him and accepted him, he gave the right to become children of God." —NLT

John 3:16 "For God so loved the world that he gave his one and only Son, that whoever believes in him shall not perish but have eternal life." —NIV

Growth

Hydrate me with your spirit
Water this soul
You plant the seed, Lord
You cause it to grow into something
Something so beautiful
I was a seed in my mother's womb
Now I'm becoming a garden
Bearing much fruit in love
Each fruit was for when I obeyed your word
Take and eat, Lord
It's all yours
I belong to you
The root is strong
The soil is rich
Grounded in your word
Come and taste the victories
That you have done through me.

Psalm 139:13-14 "For you created my inmost being; you knit me together in my mother's womb. I praise you because I am fearfully and wonderfully made; your works are wonderful, I know that full well." —NIV

Psalm 139:15 "My frame was not hidden from you when I was made in the secret place when I was woven together in the depths of the earth. Your eyes saw my unformed body; all the days ordained for me were written in your book before one of them came to be." —NIV

Matthew 13:23 "The seed that fell on good soil represents those who truly hear and understand God's word and produce a harvest of thirty, sixty, or even a hundred times as much as had been planted!" —NLT

Dear Younger Me

You hated your reflection
Sexual perversion corrupted you from an early age
You walked around acting tough
Disengaged with those around you
Walls came up
And you didn't understand the wickedness of the evil in
the world
If only you knew God had a plan
Multiple times your body was misused as a ruse
Swallowed some pills and drank to try and get rid of the
inward bruise
Just wanted to be numb
The light has been shining in different places since I was
young
He showed me different signs during different times
My flesh was blind, but my spirit was curious
Thought about things that kids didn't think about
Like life after death and why we are here in the first place
Wondering if God even noticed my face
A God that wants a relationship with the human race?
It sounded too good to be true.
Dear Younger Me,
You didn't have to be so unkind to yourself.
Why did you crave so much affection in the wrong
directions?
You were unique, full of life and compassion
Why did you allow them to dim your light?
You were meant to shine bright
I wish you would've loved yourself better
You didn't have to go with him to feel good
Those hits you took were falsified happiness
When the lows came, you experienced sadness

Then you hit repeat, and again it began
The endless cycle of shame you swam
Dear younger me,
There is a man who always had a plan over your life
He carried a heavy cross
Crown of thorns He had worn that pierced into His skull
His clothes were torn. And abused he was
Lashes this man took that made his flesh rip
Sweats of blood. He did drip
As He pleaded for that cup of suffering to leave
But the Father's plan of salvation He chose to cleave
For the joy set before Him
He endured Golgotha's hill
He wasn't satisfied until
The journey was complete
When the soldiers came in for the kill
His blood did spill
But not a bone on Him was broken
Three days later, this man rose from death
Fresh breath entered Him as He awoken
As He resurrected and conquered sin and infirmity
To offer someone like you eternity
To bring in many sons and daughters
This is why He was slaughtered
Dear younger me,
One day you will be saved
Your story will bring hope
You will rise up from that grave
The truth of Him you will crave
The word of your testimony is how you will overcome
And by the blood of the lamb, you have won
Dear younger me,
You'll be full of joy
Smile you will

As you reflect on this man
Tangible, true joy
The meaning of life you will find
Dear younger me
Dear younger me.

Romans 8:28-30 "And we know that in all things God works for the good of those who love him, who have been called according to his purpose. For those God foreknew he also predestined to be conformed to the image of his Son, that he might be the firstborn among many brothers and sisters. And those he predestined, he also called; those he called, he also justified; those he justified, he also glorified." —NIV

Royalty

I came to you naked and exposed
Now I'm clothed in your royal robes
I'm a child of the king!
Not the enemy's plaything
You have washed me in identity
You're my serenity
Freedom, you have set me free!
I will meditate on this truth
I will receive your freedom
I will ABIDE and not STRIVE
No more self-righteous pride
I get it, dad
To be loved and known by you is the greatest joy of all
I receive, I receive
Do all that you want to do
You who are faithful and true
Jesus, how you love me, and how I love you!

Galatians 5:1 "It is for freedom that Christ has set us free. Stand firm, then, and do not let yourselves be burdened again by a yoke of slavery." —NIV

John 15:9 "Just as the Father has loved Me, I have also loved you; abide in My love." —NASB 1995

Psalm 119:15 "I will meditate on your precepts and fix my eyes on your ways." —ESV

Wolves in Sheep's Clothing

I don't want to lay here and think
These deep diluted thoughts
I know I should not
But strange things have been happening
Wolves in sheep's clothing mess with my mind
How did I get to this place?
I need to sit back and rewind
From the time I got saved till now
Time to examine me in the faith
At first, your promises to me were like vows
I don't know who to trust anymore
I came to leaders seeking help
And a strange turn of events unfold
No longer leaving them untold
Why did they turn so cold?
I should've felt it wasn't genuine
I cry out to you, God
Asking you to show me who is real and what is truth
Show me God, who is bearing real fruit?
Do they even make you their root?
I seek protection
From all this deception
My Spirit needs a resurrection
All I ask is to feel warm and safe
A leader to create a suitable space
But you alone Lord is that place
I belong only in your embrace
You're the one that points me in the right direction
Now I must guard my heart because I've experienced deceit
Im sensitive and scared
Feeling impaired

Not built like others
I'm made differently
I take things to heart
I wanted to stay there
But I might need a fresh start
One day I will walk in the wholeness of your healing Lord
Man will break your heart and fail you
Yes, even those who preach His love
They're not your Lords
Don't put hope in the vanity of man
God is the chief cornerstone
Glory and honor and power be to Him alone
Trust in the Lord with all your might
Because false prophets come to bite and devour
Be watchful during this dark hour
Use wisdom to discern the days ahead
Christ only is to be your daily bread
So cling to the Lord while He may be found
Give us insight, oh God, to see in the Spirit
Protect us from the evil one, I pray
And keep our hearts from growing cold
May we be like that parable of old
The one of the sower
May we be that seed that will grow a hundred times what
was sown
For the thorns try to choke and destroy
So Lord, deploy your heartfelt encouragement
My soul needs your nourishment
Heal this hole in my heart
My God, My God
Lead me into your truth
For you are the living proof of everlasting life.

1 Timothy 4:1-2 "Now the Holy Spirit tells us clearly that in the last times some will turn away from the true faith; they will follow deceptive spirits and teachings that come from demons. These people are hypocrites and liars, and their consciences are dead." —NLT

Matthew 7:15-16 "Watch out for false prophets. They come to you in sheep's clothing, but inwardly they are ferocious wolves. By their fruit you will recognize them." —NIV

Matthew 23:9-12 "But you are not to be called 'Rabbi,' for you have one Teacher, and you are all brothers. And do not call anyone on earth 'father,' for you have one Father, and he is in heaven. Nor are you to be called instructors, for you have one Instructor, the Messiah. The greatest among you will be your servant. For those who exalt themselves will be humbled, and those who humble themselves will be exalted." —NIV

1 John 2:27 "But you have received the Holy Spirit, and he lives within you, so you don't need anyone to teach you what is true. For the Spirit teaches you everything you need to know, and what he teaches is true—it is not a lie. So just as he has taught you, remain in fellowship with Christ." —NLT

Compelled

The love of Christ compels me
Kiss me with the kisses of your mouth
Heal my broken wings
Mend these hurting things
Inside me
Revive me
Areas that I'm scared
Places that I am unaware
Rid the fears, my dear Lord
I'll follow you wherever you go
Though it feels like I'm falling apart
I know in this season, you're giving me a fresh start
Chase the little foxes away
My great shepherd
For you care about your flock
Jesus, you alone are my rock.

Psalm 61:2 "From the end of the earth I call to you when my heart is faint. Lead me to the rock that is higher than I" —ESV

Song of Songs 1:7 "Tell me, you whom my soul loves, where you pasture your flock, where you make it lie down at noon; for why should I be like one who veils herself beside the flocks of your companions?" —ESV

Song of Songs 2:15 "Catch the foxes for us, the little foxes that spoil the vineyards, for our vineyards are in blossom." —ESV

Woman of God

She is a woman of noble character
She is beautiful
She is beautiful to Him
And that's all that matters
Her arms carry her children
She is determined
Her mind is set
She has more knowledge than the learned
And her spirit much discernment
Trials and tribulations have come
But storms have ceased in her favor
The Lord has seen all of her hard labor
He's shown her He is her Savior
A woman of grace and courage
A woman I adore
A woman many look up to
I can assure
A true sister
I love her deeply; I love her dearly; I do
Laughter that is contagious, laughter that feels new
I hope that when you see yourself
You see Him encouraging you too
Smell the Lily of the valley
Let His fragrance overtake you
Laugh in His presence
Laugh at no fear of the future to come
He says, "remember the faith you had when you were young?"
"Watch me now rid of all these that have made you feel numb
Each battle you have faced, I have won
I am the lamb for you, the lion in you that has overcome

Every day you're becoming brand new I am the essence restoring you
This is true".

Proverbs 31:30: "Charm is deceptive, and beauty is fleeting; but a woman who fears the Lord is to be praised. —NIV

False Accusations

(A poem written after having false accusations come up against me from believers)

I've been depressed
I've been a mess
I can't rest
Reverting to my old ways made me feel sick
I can't tolerate it any longer
God help me be stronger
Being in the world trying to rebel
The devil is trying to get me to be under his spell
God save me from this prison cell
Break open
I no longer want to dwell in this agony
If it wasn't for my high priest interceding
I'd be left out here bleeding
He's the only one I need
Pleading to the Father for my life
Sometimes you have to make a choice
When you feel that conviction, lean in and listen
Sometimes Christians will hurt you most
Their words pierce like a sword
Especially when they swear they love the Lord
I don't understand
But I know God got a plan
I'm tired of having this fear of man
David felt the betrayal too
Those closest to him didn't stick through
Generals go through trials
If it were easy, it wouldn't be worthwhile
Get up, child smile
You are counted worthy of God

Through the confusion and chaos
Don't let the enemy rob
The joy of your salvation
I'm out here questioning everything
Wake up church in the west
Because you haven't done your best
You preach love and power
But there's no substance, no action in this hour
How will you be ready when revival hits?
Do you say you want the Holy Spirit in your midst?
But you're poor
Wretched
Blind and naked
Yeah, I've been hurt
Had moms and fathers
Sisters and brothers say that they love me
Only to cut me off based on what they've heard
False accusations against me
Not living out the truth of the word
My soul is filled with doubt
I'm left here without
Phone calls, text messages
Man
Did the early church really exist?
Those in the book of Acts
I wish it were here in my midst
Those living as one, so united in love
I have to ask, is there any genuine love out there?
Anyone who cares?
Life isn't fair
I'm sure some people practice what they preach
But I have yet to see it
I'm so sick of the church
These four walls

Sometimes those who claim to love God can be the fakest
people you'll meet
Self-righteous religious zealots
Not trying to resolve issues
I'm here using a thousand tissues
Tears dripping down
Trying not to drown in this sorrow
I still love Jesus
I've got my faith
There's a glimmer of hope on the inside
It won't let me die
He's telling me to stay alive
Though it feels hard to try
And my spirit is dry
Man will fail you
But He never will
I'm breaking away
There's nothing left to say
It doesn't matter what people think anymore, anyway
I'm seeking approval from the Father alone He is my
home.

Psalm 41:9 "Even my close friend, someone I trusted, one
who shared my bread, has turned against me." —NIV

Matthew 5:23-24 "Therefore, if you are offering your gift
at the altar and there remember that your brother or sister
has something against you, leave your gift there in front
of the altar. First go and be reconciled to them; then come
and offer your gift." —NIV

Jealousy Is A Thief
In The Church

Why are you after titles?
Don't you know they're idols?
He's coming back for a spotless bride
Pure and refined
Get out of this bind
Jesus, purify us!
Oh Jesus!
It's too much
You're such a Holy one.
Prostrated before you.
Crying out for purity
Crying out for unity!
Crying for us to all desire to be like you!
Truth and righteousness
It hungers and thirsts me
How you love your children
It grieves your heart to watch your body quarrel
If you can't stand united now
How will you stand on the day of my return, oh my body?
Don't be shoddy
Lest the envy divides you all
Whoever abides in the Son
Will overflow with love
Please don't be jealous; my kids
Only zealous to love
I make room for the gifts in you
I'm the one that lifts you up in your calling
And keeps you from falling Who desires to be great?
Let them lay down their life
Repent of the strife within yourselves

For the Son of man did not come to be served but to serve
I did not claim all that I did deserve
Did you not read about my life on earth?
I washed my beloved one's feet
Whom among you are meek?
I know it can feel weak
Being considered the scum
And holding your tongue
When you think you're entitled to it all
Not everyone follows the call
Oh, be like me
It is the only way to be free
The only way you will clearly see
Tears may fall
You'll feel so small
All alone, like you're hitting a wall
People will make comments
Even your own brothers and sisters
But know that everything you do is unto me
Bless and pray for those who treat you unfairly
I surround you
Other's opinions don't amount to what I say Is it not what
I see that counts?
I see the unseen
What no one else notices
Let all that you do be unto the Lord
Serving unto Him is your great reward!
The joy in Him is more incredible than earthly pleasures
Forever and ever
As you're being purified, love will consume you
The pride will subside
Oh my bride
How beautiful I will make you in my eyes
Lay your flesh aside

And allow me to reside fully
You'll be baptized in my GREAT love
And be gentle as doves.

Matthew 20:28 "just as the Son of Man did not come to be served, but to serve, and to give his life as a ransom for many." —NIV

Philippians 2:5-8 " In your relationships with one another have the same mindset as Christ Jesus: Who, being in very nature God, did not consider equality with God something to be used to his own advantage; rather, he made himself nothing by taking the very nature of a servant, being made in human likeness. And being found in appearance as a man, he humbled himself by becoming obedient to death—even death on a cross! —NIV

Galatians 1:10 "For am I now seeking the approval of man, or of God? Or am I trying to please man? If I were still trying to please man, I would not be a servant of Christ." —ESV

Living Water

Water refreshes
It gives life
It cleanses
It hydrates
Jesus is the living water
From His well, one can drink freely
From His well, one will never thirst again
Come all you weary
Drink from this living well
The wellsprings of life
The refreshing waters of the living God
Once parched, now quenched
My spirit is no longer dry
Once dead, now revived
I no longer need to try
My God is alive
He is the waters many refuse know
Living waters only some He will show
And those who chose to partake in the mysteries of Christ
His soul He will make awake to the meaning of life
Why wrestle with the truth?
Put down those fists
God is in your midst
See as He persists for your soul?
Don't turn away and grow cold
Chose the living water
This is the Fathers heart
From the start
To bring in many sons and daughters
Oh, Come to the waters.

Isaiah 55:1 "Come, all you who are thirsty,
come to the waters;
and you who have no money, come, buy and eat!
Come, buy wine and milk without money and without
cost." —NIV

Isaiah 55:6-7 "Seek the Lord while he may be found; call
on him while he is near. Let the wicked forsake their ways
and the unrighteous their thoughts.
Let them turn to the Lord, and he will have mercy on
them, and to our God, for he will freely pardon" —NIV

John 4:10 "Jesus answered her, "If you knew the gift of
God and who it is that asks you for a drink, you would
have asked him, and he would have given you living
water." —NIV

John 4:14 "but whoever drinks the water I give them will
never thirst. Indeed, the water I give them will become in
them a spring of water welling up to eternal life." —NIV

Church Hurt

(A poem written after being cut off ungodly by church leaders)

I feel so small
As I stare into this wall
Why do I stall
Daydreaming
Tears streaming
Gleaning to the glimmer of hope I have left in you, God
Why have they forsaken me?
The mother I thought you gifted me with
My whole family
Left alone, I am
Deserted
They said I subverted them
My patience is wearing thin
This pain is crawling in my skin
Itching within
Will I ever win?
The pain God. The pain.
Two years of my life, I gave that place
I feel like a disgrace
Humiliated and beaten down
I can't seem to turn that frown upside down
I drown in sorrow
They took me under their wings
I got healing
I thought you used them to do all those deep things within me
But now I have to go search for a new home
But God
I feel anxiety now when I step foot in a church

And I'm prone to roam
I wish they would pick up the phone and make things right
I can't stay too long, my heart beats, and my chest feels tight
I feel everyone new that I meet will hurt me too
Cant get stuck to people again like glue
Putting up so many walls
I now need therapy, you see
I have trauma from all the drama this has caused
Have you ever been hurt by an institution?
Please tell me, what's the solution?
Jesus, please make restitution on my behalf
Help me to pray for their absolution
I don't want any more worldly substitutions that numb my pain
Break these chains before I go insane
I know the enemy is to blame
He thinks he can get away with this game
But in the end, he loses
God, I speak against disunity
And I declare unity
Help, Lord
Do not let this situation become my downfall
Come and squander this Holy Spirit
Once and for all
In your name Lord, I trust in and call.

I wrote this after being shunned by a church that has cult-like traits. I did not know they were like a cult until I left. I sadly did not realize how controlling and dominating they were until they excommunicated me. I was so embarrassed to tell my family and friends about it. But

I found I have had a more profound sense of healing in talking about what I've been through. If a controlling institution has hurt you, do not give up hope, beloved. God is grieved to see you wounded and how you were treated unjustly. They will have to give an account to Him for not making things suitable with you in a biblical way. Do not isolate and allow the enemy to win. Take the ground and reclaim who you are in Christ. If you give up, they win, and so does the accuser. So rise, child of God. He's not done with you yet, and God will use your pain to encourage others. Just as Joseph said in Genesis (Genesis 50:20 "You intended to harm me, but God intended it for good to accomplish what is now being done, the saving of many lives." —NIV)

Though they meant it for evil, God will turn it around and use it for good. You are a voice to the voiceless, and your testimony will bring encouragement and hope to the hopeless.
Matthew 5:23 "Therefore, if you are offering your gift at the altar and there remember that your brother or sister has something against you, leave your gift there in front of the altar. First, go and be reconciled to them; then come and offer your gift." —NIV

Luke 17:1-4 "Jesus said to his disciples: "Things that cause people to stumble are bound to come, but woe to anyone through whom they come. It would be better for them to be thrown into the sea with a millstone tied around their neck than to cause one of these little ones to stumble. So watch yourselves. –NIV

Luke 17:3-4 "If your brother or sister] sins against you, rebuke them; and if they repent, forgive them. Even if they sin against you seven times in a day and seven times come back to you saying 'I repent,' you must forgive them." —NIV

Matthew 6:15 "But if you do not forgive others their sins, your Father will not forgive your sins." —NIV

Nana

(Dedicated to my grandmother)

As I look at my grandmother, I realize how short life is
Simply staring at her causes a spiral of emotions to burst
within
I walk away and cry because I know time is thin
I wish I could keep you forever
Our bond is unique; our bond runs deep
I don't know how I'll ever handle losing you
You're my favorite person ever
When I think of you these days, I weep
I sit up at night crying and interceding for you I tell
Jesus to please never leave nor forsake you
Will there really be a day when there will be no death?
A day where God will resurrect all the elect?
A day with no sickness or pain?
A day where we will never take His love in vain?
A paradise where we will all gain eternity
To be with loved ones forever will be our certainty
I long for that day
It seems so far away
For now, it pains my heart to think of the ones I love
seeing decay
It's confusing to love others because you know one day
they'll die
I can't even lie; I think, "what's the point"?
You have to make a choice to latch or detach
It's a choice I wrestle with
A restless match
A lonely life of pushing people away and not having to feel
pain when they're gone?
Or a life of loving and feeling anguish when they perish?

How can I cherish the moments without overthinking?
I must confess, this mess of life causes me distress
Perhaps I think too deeply?
Jesus, help me surrender these thoughts to you
Render my heart to your perfect peace and love
Calm my anxieties
Please help me to keep loving and not give up
I feel the walls forming again
I want these thoughts to end
I can't control the outcome of life
Bring down this strife my mind is having with you
Pull me out of this hole I'm digging myself in
Make my soul whole in you
And show me, my God
That You alone are in control.

Psalm 90:12 "Teach us to number our days, that we may gain a heart of wisdom." —NIV

Psalm 94:19 "When anxiety was great within me, your consolation brought me joy." —NIV

Psalm 56:8 "Record my misery; list my tears on your scroll — are they not in your record?" —NIV

Faithful Shepherd

My love is weak now
But you love me anyway
Your presence is strong
God, I've been so wrong
Please be my friend
You're the only one that stays true till the end
My one and only
Fill the room
Cancel the gloom
I'm scared and feel so small
Afraid of the future and everything that seems so far away
It's hard to glean on your promises
And live for today
Why do you tug at my heart so much?
Then leave me without physical touch?
Can't you feel my need for you?
I know you've called me to stay
But I want to isolate
Why do I want to run away?
Everything within me screams out for you
I am nothing
And I have nothing to give
Just an empty vessel
Sometimes barely want to live
In need of you to fill me up
Cause me to overflow

Here I am, God
My heart laid out on the floor
Everything that I am and more belongs to you
These rough edges are coming undone
Great I am

Remind me who I am
Where is this man I'm longing for?
Jesus touch me to my core
I implore I need so much more
What is real love?
Can you show me?
You show up now!
I see you
Exposing the dark
And illuminating my surroundings with the light of your love
Jesus, you're beautiful!
I Love You, Jesus!
He carries healing!
He is the healer and lifter of my countenance!
You're my strength!
My deliverer!
My helper!
My Shepherd is beautiful!
More lovely than all the others
He leads with mercy and grace
He leads with kindness
Gentle and warm
I want His embrace!
Fire in His eyes
And glory on His face!
Time with you is sweet.
I lean in and listen.
For I know what you have to say is deep
Thank you for your goodness God
Your faithfulness is unending
I used to live away from you, pretending
That everything was alright
But deep down inside, there was much fright
Away from you is where I never want to be again

How are you so kind to me?
I feel like it never ends.
I don't deserve it
Yet you made a way so I could be worth it
The 99 for the 1?
Loving me before time has even begun? Who am I in your sight?
You shine so brightly
My heart can't comprehend
How you've brought me back
You could've let me go forever
But you're jealous for me, God
Your goodness loves and disciplines
It hems me in
Now in you, I am strong
You've shown me your heart is my home, its where I belong
I cry as I write these words
I don't understand how you love so much
After I walked away, I was pretty sure there were others you would have preferred over me.
I'm still imperfect, and always will be
Impatient, frustrated, and angry some days
Too tired to go on
Trying to command my mind to get out of this confusing daze
Feeling like I'm in a restless maze
Running through obstacles
Looking for your rest
My blemishes make me feel unqualified and stressed
Dark but lovely?
When will I feel fully alive?
I want to understand how to live for you
I need to learn how to abide and not strive
You're breaking the pride

And tearing down every lie
It's not anything I do or say
But what you did
God, have your way
In me
Holy Spirit
Come and display
Your glory through your servant
She's flawed, but you love her
She's defective but observant
To what your word says
She loves you too
And wants to be fully lead
By everything you say and do
Come and show me what's true
And how to fully, follow you
Though I feel like a restless wanderer
I will have a breakthrough
Oh God, when will you answer?
The mental confusion exhausts me
Am I talking to a wall?
Even though I feel you are silent,
I will choose to love you, LORD
I choose to live for you!
Your hand is upon me.
I am consecrated for you
You lift me from the ground!
You spin me around
You cause me to soar!
I will roar of your goodness.
These broken wings are learning to fly into your love again!
You're getting rid of those foxes and things.
I look forward to the day when we will laugh and dance
together

Longing to fellowship with you, Abba!
Come and fill my empty space, Jesus!
Until the world no longer has a trace in me.

Psalm 23:5 "You prepare a table before me in the presence of my enemies. You anoint my head with oil; my cup overflows." —NIV

SOS 2:15 "Catch the foxes for us, The little foxes that are ruining the vineyards, While our vineyards are in blossom." —NASB

Hebrews 13:6 "So we can say with confidence, "The LORD is my helper, so I will have no fear. What can mere people do to me?" —NLT

Psalm 119:19 "I am a stranger on earth; do not hide your commands from me." —NIV

Song of Solomon 1:5 "I am very dark, but lovely, O daughters of Jerusalem, like the tents of Kedar, like the curtains of Solomon." —ESV

Jeremiah 31:3 "The LORD appeared to us in the past, saying: "I have loved you with an everlasting love; I have drawn you with unfailing kindness." —NIV

Matthew 18:12 "What do you think? If a man has a hundred sheep, and one of them has gone astray, does he not leave the ninety-nine on the mountains and go in search of the one that went astray? —ESV

Giver

I trust in you
Not the amount
I have in my account
Like that copper coin
Giving all I have that's in my heart
Believing you to impart your provision
As I make a decision
To not worry about tomorrow
The days have troubles of their own
For you say to seek first your kingdom
And its righteousness
Lord, as I've grown in my faith
You've shown your providence
God, you care about my motive
You look to see if I trust in myself
Or in you who gives like no one else
So I choose to live by faith
For freely I have received, and freely I shall give.

Mark 12:43-44: "Calling his disciples to him, Jesus said, "Truly I tell you, this poor widow has put more into the treasury than all the others. They all gave out of their wealth; but she, out of her poverty, put in everything—all she had to live on." —NIV.

Matthew 6:33-34: "Seek the Kingdom of God above all else, and live righteously, and he will give you everything you need. "So don't worry about tomorrow, for tomorrow will bring its own worries. Today's trouble is enough for today. —NLT

Broken

(Because of the fall, we are all broken, wounded vessels. Born into sin and broken humanity. Feeling our brokenness can make us lose heart, even to the point of losing our will to live. A poem about how Jesus meets us in our wounded state and fills us with true love, which restores meaning and purpose)

We are all broken
None of us are fixed
One of us to the next
We are all left amiss
Broken families
Broken dreams
Generational curses
How can we be redeemed?
The pride of our hearts
It holds us back from truly accepting love
And giving back
Instead, we allow the attack
Of the enemy
To mess with us
He blinds our eyes
So we cant see
And fills us with lies
With his little spies
We are leaning toward destruction
The issues we have
We turn our heads
Instead of fixing them
We want to leave them unsaid
When will it stop?
From one father to the next
When will it end?

I can't pretend
That it's alright
Men will fail you
Those you look up to
They're all broken too
There's no one left anymore
Nothing left to do
No father or mother figure to trust
They all failed me
And they'll fail you to
Be careful what you make your foundation
Remember, Jesus is the only salvation
Sometimes I feel like I'm coming to the end
There doesn't seem much left to mend
I want to pretend no longer
Sometimes I want to say bye
Oh, these deep things that I feel
It's just too real
I'm not made of steel
It's who I am
Oh, Son of man
I've tried, and I've tried
But I feel you aren't there, God
It's just not fair
My heart can't take
All this loneliness that's at stake
It hurts too much
I shouldn't have made them my crutch
The tears fall
As I crawl and try to find breath
But all I can feel around me is death
It creeps up on me
This is where I come to the end of my scene
I've tried to glean on you, God

But I feel like you just beat me with your rod
I have nothing to lean on
I'm gone
Maybe one day I'll be okay
Maybe one day, I'll feel like I can stay
One day I won't want to walk away
But that day isn't today
I want to be left here to decay
We all will anyways
Who's to stay?

But wait
As I feel I'm coming to the end of myself
Here in this darkness
When I think I can't see I feel the warmth of His light now
Shining on me! No need to strife on my own anymore I
put down that knife!
In my flesh, I'm so deficient.
But you tell me your grace is sufficient!
You're pulling me through.
The shackles and chains are being destroyed
My insides no longer feel void!
I'm set free!
What perfect love is this?
This whole time I wasn't left amiss!
My whole life, in my heart, I felt there was a dent
But you always cared
You were always there
Just waiting for me to repent!
The son of man is breaking through
I'm brand new!
You tell me that I'm forever found in you!

Psalm 34:8 "The Lord is close to the brokenhearted and saves those who are crushed in spirit." —NIV.

Psalm 43:5 "Why, my soul, are you downcast? Why so disturbed within me? Put your hope in God, for I will yet praise him, my Savior and my God." —NIV.

Clinic

19 years old
It's cold outside, and I don't want to do this
His friend is there and greets me with a kiss
Air is what I need, but I could care less about myself
Waiting in the room to go in
Told to swallow some pills, and the kill will begin
Second thoughts, but he calls me and says I have to go
through with it
Pill number one
(gulp)
Pill number two
(gulp)
A rush into the bathroom
You leave out of me
I look down, and a mini-me is what I see
What have I done?
Why have I hit up that clinic?
Oh no
I regret this
Why didn't they tell me that I'd regret it?
Why did they teach me it's not a life yet?
I thought it was a safer bet
But
I don't feel better yet
I lost a part of my soul
It left
Insides are ripped
And he dipped
Unborn baby
Do you think maybe you can come back to mommy?
No
In the end, it wasn't worth it

You would've been ten
I wish I could've stopped me then
I'll never forget that day
That you went away
I'll grieve you till I decay
The School system led me astray
It failed me and made me think it was okay
Brainwashed into what life meant
My worldview bent
I'm so discontent
I wish I would've spent more time contemplating that decision
What a derision
Doctors, how could you work there?
Nurses, don't you even care?
You have blood on your hands
Who will rise up in the system?
What will it take God for them to listen!
They're allowing murder to take place
Day in and day out
It's a disgrace
How we degrade the human race
God brought me to my face, and I repented
That is why He relented
He spared me
But that sin is ever before me
I wish it weren't legal
I wish I weren't even allowed to have ever walked into a place like that!
Oh, the attack on this generation
Triggered and crying immensely
So hard to write these words
Why people?
Wake up!

What are you doing?
It is murder
It is wrong
When you have a personal experience, you know firsthand
That little life isn't something bland
I want my baby back
I want my baby back
I want my baby back
I want my baby back
I want my baby back
He or she was real!
I don't care what the system tries to indoctrinate you with
People, we are going to be judged for allowing this wickedness to continue on our land
Oh America
And nations of the world
Wake up
This is murder
This is murder
God open up blind eyes
Please help them to understand
Oh Lord God Almighty
Could you help us to take a stand?
A stand for life
And may you, Lord
Disband the plan of the enemy
And His wicked schemes
All this madness is too extreme
The people are indoctrinated, it seems
Lord Jesus Christ
Come and redeem life
This madness is becoming out of hand
Oh the guilt
Oh, the blood being spilled on this land

You're the only man that can save and rescue
So come quick and do not delay
Do something in our day
I hope and pray.

Habakkuk 1:2 "How long, O LORD, must I call for help? But you do not listen!
"Violence is everywhere!" I cry, but you do not come to save." —NLT

Psalm 32:3-5 "When I kept silent, my bones wasted away through my groaning all day long. For day and night, your hand was heavy on me; my strength was sapped as in the heat of summer. Then I acknowledged my sin to you and did not cover up my iniquity. I said, "I will confess my transgressions to the Lord." And you forgave the guilt of my sin."—NIV

Psalm 51:3 "For I know my transgressions, and my sin is always before me." —NIV

Psalm 51:13-14 "Restore to me the joy of your salvation, and make me willing to obey you. Then I will teach your ways to rebels, and they will return to you. Forgive me for shedding blood, O God who saves; then I will joyfully sing of your forgiveness." —NLT

For Victims of Human trafficking

My heart is heavy
Deep breaths as I toss and turn
Its 5 am, and I have chest pains
My heart is pounding; it burns
I yearn for justice
The colors of the world are escaping me
Hyperventilating
These children have it bad
Listen as I put all this information on blast
I've lost hope in humanity
Too much depravity
I feel like I'm getting a taste of insanity
The children are screaming
The demons are pounding
Listen to me as I begin expounding
Watch your surroundings
They're locked in a cage, being abused
Day and night, living in fearful fright
How can you not feel enraged?
What if it was your child?
Would you then pray and engage in this warfare?
What will it take for all of us to wake up
And partner with God to bring down these principalities
Please, the children need to be saved from these abnormalities!
I won't stop until I go down to my grave
Jesus said to pray
So on my knees, I get
Yeah, I'm upset
You might think what I'm about to say is insane I bet

The deep state is corrupt
All this injustice will soon one day from the surface erupt
They disrupt the people and lead them away from my steeple
They cause madness and upheaval
The masses are blind; they've all lost their minds
No one wants the truth
No one seeks to find
Who loves it?
Being led by the media's words
Spoon fed with all that's absurd
After He called me, I upped and left my comfort and clung to His word
I stopped covering my ears and deserted the world
I don't care anymore if I die trying to bring change
People need to wake up; no more playing games
It's time to rearrange the order of society
Time to ruffle the feathers
I'm ready to stir the pot
To tear at the fabric of an institution will be my lot
They'll all be opposed to a fresh wind
I'm ready to spill the truth
Now I'll begin
Baal worship didn't perish; it's still evident today
Masquerading in Hollywood and on the left, it's on full display
I know it's hard to hear what I have to say
It was for me, too, at first I had a lot of fear
But once I came near to Jesus and inclined my ear
I could feel in my spirit ever so clear not to turn away anymore
Who will speak for the children, the blood being spilled?
And all of the murders that
No one goes further to investigate

Doesn't that make you wonder?
And why did certain famous people die right before they were about to expose something that no one knew?
They were on the verge of revealing a ring of pedophiles
So close to exposing all the files
And a particular actor who called these perverts out
Clearly stated in a video that he was not suicidal without a doubt
He exposed another actor for being a pervert, among other names
Shortly after his video of these claims, he "jumped off of a bridge."
Ruling as a suicide
Who is killing these people?
What are these perverts trying to hide?
They're trying to escape from people trying to pry
Hollywood is now getting nervous because people are waking up and beginning to scratch the surface
How about another man's claims?
Stating, "Hollywood is an institutionalized pedophile ring. They use and abuse kids for their own sick spiritual beliefs. They harvest these kids for their energy and feast on their blood. They don't do it mercifully; they scare them before they sacrifice them. The more innocent the child, the more terrified they are, the more they thrive on it".
No wonder they are trying to silence Trump as he drains the nasty swamp
Do you think Jeffrey Epstein really killed himself?
He had dirt on all these people on his shelf
The elite that visited his sex island
Get stirred and don't believe the lies!
Think for yourself, don't allow ignorance to be your demise
We need to stop living in disguise

Everyone thought the prophets of the old testament were insane too
They were outcasts that society didn't want anything to do with
They were the only ones speaking the truth
And they were killed for it
If Jesus died for being honest
What do you think they'll do to you?
Don't fear, though; it's okay.
It's our destiny to be with Him for all of our days
Fear Him only who can kill the body and soul and send him to hell
Not him who can kill your flesh but your spirit; he cant dwell
You're living for eternity; open your hearts to this certainty
Be a voice that will rise above the noise
A voice that won't conform to the pressures of society
Let the truth be your sobriety What are you living for?
Being a slave to the world no more
I don't understand why bad things happen
But I know what happens at the end of His book
I've had a look
More will be exposed
Soon, justice will come for the wicked scum
Hell is their destination
Unless they repent
It is their sum.

Leviticus 28:21 "Do not permit any of your children to be offered as a sacrifice to Molech, for you must not bring shame on the name of your God. I am the Lord." —NLT

Jeremiah 15:17 "I never joined the people in their merry feasts. I sat alone because your hand was on me. I was filled with indignation at their sins." —NLT.

2 kings 17:16-17 "They forsook all the commands of the LORD their God and made for themselves two idols cast in the shape of calves, and an Asherah pole. They bowed down to all the starry hosts, and they worshiped Baal. They sacrificed their sons and daughters in the fire. They practiced divination and sought omens and sold themselves to do evil in the eyes of the LORD, arousing his anger. —NIV

Ephesians 6:12 "For we do not wrestle against flesh and blood, but against the rulers, against the authorities, against the cosmic powers over this present darkness, against the spiritual forces of evil in the heavenly places. —ESV

Revelation 6:12 "They shouted to the Lord and said, "O Sovereign Lord, holy and true, how long before you judge the people who belong to this world and avenge our blood for what they have done to us?" —NLT.

Deuteronomy 32:35 "Vengeance is mine, and recompense, for the time when their foot shall slip; for the day of their calamity is at hand, and their doom comes swiftly.' —ESV

Hope

Hope.
Hope as things get darker.
Hope as wickedness and sin increase.
Hope because I know who wins in the end.
Oh, the intimacy.
Where the finger of God will personally wipe away the tears of the eyes of those who have overcome by the blood of the lamb and by the word of their testimony.
This is a promise for the children of God alone.
A promise for those who wholeheartedly decide to follow Jesus in righteousness and truth.
For those whom He has purchased as His own, with His blood.
If you want this blessed assurance, put your Hope in Jesus today.
There is no time to delay.
He is the living Hope, the only way, the truth, and the life.
Once you put your faith in Him, you have an eternal hope, the Holy Spirit living inside of you to comfort you in all circumstances no matter the trials that are to come.
Because beloved things will only get worse, and darkness will only continue to increase.
But those who hope in their God will not be shaken up by the world. (Psalm 112:6, " Surely the righteous will never be shaken; they will be remembered forever. —NIV)

Those who love their God will have the privilege of being known by Him and personally touched by Him.
How I long to see this day.
It brings tears to my eyes.
Just envisioning His hands touching my face.
Touching those who love Him.

Touching those who are willing to die for Him.
Touching those who don't deny Him in persecuted countries, no matter how badly they're tortured for the name of Christ. Gently wiping away their tears.

Oh, come, Lord Jesus.
Make us sober-minded.
Touch us.
Maranatha, come.

John 14:6 "Jesus answered, "I am the way and the truth and the life. No one comes to the Father except through me." —NIV.

2 Corinthians 1:3-4 "Praise be to the God and Father of our Lord Jesus Christ, the Father of compassion and the God of all comfort, who comforts us in all our troubles so that we can comfort those in any trouble with the comfort we ourselves receive from God." —NIV

1 Corinthians 16:22-23 "if anyone does not love the Lord, he is to be accursed.
Maranatha! The grace of the Lord Jesus be with you." —NASB

A Dance With My King

Let me dance with you, my king
Let this be our love song
It's only you and me, only you and me
Hold me a little closer
Cause my steps to align with yours
Take my hand
Spin me through life's journeys
I'm found in you
Let the music continue
Let's keep going
Hand in hand
Could you teach me how to move to your rhythm?
Caught up in this moment
Your eyes captivate me
With one glance, I'm weak
You pull me in closer
You stir up the living waters within me
I can't take it; I'm breathless
I don't want this moment to end
I'm forever yours
Tears flow down my eyes
The music is ending
You tell me you'll be back
Next time we'll dance together in your new paradise
Beautifully prepared for us coming down from heaven
Till then, my beautiful king
Goodnight, for now, goodnight for now.

SOS 8:6 "Set me as a seal upon your heart, as a seal upon your arm, for love is strong as death, jealousy is fierce as the grave.
Its flashes are flashes of fire, the very flame of the Lord."
—ESV

Hey friend

(A Psalm written for a friend that was going through a hard time, a psalm of encouragement)

Hey friend
Don't give up now
Hey friend
Look up now
He's here for you
And He sees everything that you're going through
Hey friend
You're not alone
Cause He's made your heart His home
Don't roam around in your head
Cause you'll surely drown instead
If you don't look to His word
You'll go absurd
He is revealing that what you're feeling is temporary
Look to the cross
Because without it, all hope is lost
He is the keeper of your soul
So dig deeper now
Please don't give up
Your emotions tell you one thing
But we aren't meant to live by them
Only by Him
And what He says
Make it count now
Declare
Use your voice
Love is a choice
Cause we are only here for a mist
There is a fight within you

You know it too
Don't give up now
Don't give up
I love you through thick and thin it's time for you to unleash now
The fighter within.

Job 22:28 "You will also declare a thing, And it will be established for you; So light will shine on your ways. —NKJV

Exodus 14:14 "The LORD will fight for you; you need only to be still." —NIV
Proverbs 13:12 "Hope deferred makes the heart sick, but a longing fulfilled is a tree of life." —NIV

Plow

Yes, I love thee
Like a well-watered garden in the spring
Each facet of your beauty is colorful
Beyond compare its wonderful
Let me gaze upon you in the field
I yield to this surrendered love
So sweet and innocent like a dove
Chase after me
Our hands reaching for each other
Looking to you as I lay on the grass
Oh
Please let this last
God, I love you so much
You pull me out of the fire
Saved me from the enemies spell
Allow me to drink from your well
Your grace swoops in
Once again

When I was tempted to sin
And dwell in pain
When I didn't want to feel
And all my energy was drained

Exhaustion and tears
Lost for words
Saying, "It's been how many years?"
Then I hear a voice that speaks ever so clearer
"I am here, my dear
Instructing you and guiding your heart
No one shines like me
Incline your ear

Come near
My truth will set you free
This love I have for you is stronger than the grave
I am the love that you crave
And only I can save
I am truth
Look to me
Focus your gaze now
Put your hand to the plow
And follow me."

Psalm 16:9-11 "Therefore my heart is glad and my tongue rejoices; my body also will rest secure because you will not abandon me to the realm of the dead, nor will you let your faithful one see decay. You make known to me the path of life; you will fill me with joy in your presence, with eternal pleasures at your right hand." —NIV

Luke 9:62 "But Jesus told him, "Anyone who puts a hand to the plow and then looks back is not fit for the Kingdom of God." —NLT

LOVE IS..

Love is self-sacrificing
To fully be all in for others
To let ourselves go
And allow you, Lord
To fully flow
Within us
We throw the word around all the time
But in reality, it's so conditional
When someone gets us mad, our walls come up
Pride creeps in
And hardens our hearts
Then we start to depart
From the truth of all that you are
The vows fade away
And lovers are left in dismay
So please help us to be a better generation
Shine on your bride Holy Spirit
This is my declaration
Give us a clear revelation
Make us strong
And cause us to bond
Fully in love
Unite us all
Trade away anything that is not of you
Help us live out our lives in the fullness of you
Inside and out
So all of humanity will never doubt
That you are in us
And we are one
For they will know us by our love
Rid us of ourselves
So we can be a pure reflection

To give them direction
Of how to receive you
And know you
Oh Lord our God.

"I pray that they will all be one, just as you and I are one—as you are in me, Father, and I am in you. And may they be in us so that the world will believe you sent me". John 17:21 —NLT

"Your love for one another will prove to the world that you are my disciples." -John 13:35 —NLT

"The second is this: 'Love your neighbor as yourself.' There is no commandment greater than these." -Mark 12:31 —NIV

No to Division

Left and right
Distractions to get us hyped
We're so laser-focused on being right
That we lose sight of the one true light
Jesus Christ
So no, I'm not a republican
Nor am I a democrat
I operate out of the word
Lest I go absurd
Haven't you heard?
In the beginning, was the WORD.
And the word was with God and was God
We can never restore creation
Only Jesus will one day when He sits on that throne
So stop trying to be in control
We'll only fully be at peace when we're finally home
Just as Paul preached one thing, Christ crucified
So should we
Then the lies of the unwise will evaporate
He will open up their eyes
And do away with their despise
As Christ is being preached
May the truth of His word convict
So they will no longer operate out of hate
Enough with all this endless debate
Find common ground
Time to turn things around
In Christ only are we indeed found
Holy Spirit will bring truth as He is proclaimed
Putting an end to the divisive flame
Be wise and don't use His name for an agenda
Lest shame be brought on you, and you are to blame

May the truth of what you've done alone set people free,
Lord
Use your double-edged sword
Holy Spirit, draw them to your word
Testify of Jesus
Then the blinders will open
As you've spoken, the good news
No longer will they give in to a ruse
You are enough to set them free
So come Holy Ghost, I plea.

1 Corinthians 2:2 For I determined not to know anything among you except Jesus Christ and Him crucified. —NKJV

Uncultured

(A poem about not being conformed to the culture)

Oh, Jesus, I stand with you
You've helped me with all that I've been through
You're the way, the truth, and the life
I lay myself down
I don't want any worldly crown
You only are who I want to serve
You deserve all of me and nothing less
Lord, I confess I'm not perfect, but you died so I could be worth it
In your sight
My life is in your hands
Oh great, I am
Could you help me to understand your plans? And keep me from the fear of man.

Do not conform to the pattern of this world, but be transformed by the renewing of your mind. Then you will be able to test and approve what God's will is—his good, pleasing and perfect will." -Romans 12:2 —NIV

Jesus answered, "I am the way and the truth and the life. No one comes to the Father except through me. -John 14:6 —NIV

"Don't be afraid of those who want to kill your body; they cannot touch your soul. Fear only God, who can destroy both soul and body in hell. -Matthew 10:28 —NLT

Joy for Sadness

Sadness is all you feel
You want to lay in bed
Binge watch and listen to sad tunes that get what you
mean
Suppress your feelings
You no longer dream
Inside you scream
Past memories resurface
All you do is cry all the time
Tears flow from your eyes
And the glow of your countenance fades
You're feeling low
Must hide from the world because you feel if they knew
the truth, they'd despise
The weak person you are
And all the scars you carry
You don't want to tarry
And you don't even know your worth
It's hard to breathe
Can't feel hope, don't even want to eat
As you stare at the person in the mirror
It becomes more apparent that no one understands
And you feel like God has lifted His hands
And the plans He has for your life
You're alone on your island of brokenness
Isolated and disconnected from the other lands
Your mind is detached from your surroundings
You can't seem to latch onto the real world
And you feel like you're drowning
You put your phone on airplane mode and isolate because
you feel this heavy load inside your chest.

And you don't know how else to digress or find peaceful
rest
Your mind is wandering off
Pondering a million different things
You just want to scream!
And no one seems to ring your bell
Your emotional, hiding in your shell
"Just cheer up," they say
"God heals the brokenhearted; he's bigger than your pain."
The enemy laughs as I feel lame Am I going insane?
I know what my Jesus did.
But I want to erase these feelings
I want to feel better
I feel sick
My brain is broken
I thought I was better
But it seems like I can't weather the storm
Jesus is my norm, but I can't force that smile right now
To be honest, I want to run away for miles and not come
back for awhile
And when I'm down, I have to fight the itch to not swallow
it down with something that will numb it
God help
I have to sit here and deal
Process through it and feel
I don't even want it to be real
This spiel is so hard to get
I feel so upset
I want this to go away, I do, but I must tell you what's true
I know I look like a victory
And that's what you see when you look at me
But I'm not perfect
I pressed through the pain a ton
I made a choice

To deal with these things
To use my voice and declare my identity in Christ
But others aren't so blessed, you see
And it's something I have to fight through
Wrestle with and combat
Force me to get out of bed
When I felt like I was hanging by a thread
My insides felt dead
It wasn't always like this for me though
Use to call out of work pretending I was sick
Just to have my own mental health day
I wasn't okay
And sometimes I'm still not
But Lord, you are patient
To those struggling with mental health, read these words
The Lord is patient with you in your pain, depression,
and anxiety
He knows it's not a game
Receive His patience and love
God won't give up on you
To the one who sees us at our worst
And sticks through all of our hurts
The Lord is gentle and kind
He won't give up on His chosen
You're interwoven together
And Jesus is at the right hand of the Father forever
That great High priest
To the one who talks with the Father and speaks life
over you
Generation, Jesus will fight for you
Then you will shine like Christ
Joy for Sadness in the exchange
As the Lord comes to rearrange your heart
The enemies plans will be disengaged

The Joy of the Lord will be your strength
Can you not hear Him?
That great Shepherd of the flock?
Your High Priest?
Incline your ears
He is near
Jesus is standing at the door, and He knocks
He says, "here am I."
Give Him the keys to unlock.
Be ready for your Lord's child.
Let Him open up the door to your heart
Then the healing will start
Vent to Him alone because He hears every groan
My wellspring of tears is here
Collect them with your bottle
No more isolating or holding back
The enemy won't win
I'm letting my God in!
Only Jesus can stop the bleeding inside
Just open up, allow Him to reside
To Him who can heal your pain within.

Isaiah 61:1-3 "The Spirit of the Sovereign LORD is upon me, for the LORD has anointed me to bring good news to the poor. He has sent me to comfort the brokenhearted and to proclaim that captives will be released and prisoners will be freed. He has sent me to tell those who mourn that the time of the LORD's favor has come, and with it, the day of God's anger against their enemies. To all who mourn in Israel, he will give a crown of beauty for ashes, a joyous blessing instead of mourning, festive praise instead of despair. In their righteousness, they will

be like great oaks that the LORD has planted for his own glory. —NLT

Romans 8:34 "Who then is the one who condemns? No one. Christ Jesus who died—more than that, who was raised to life—is at the right hand of God and is also interceding for us." —NIV

Hebrews 13:20-21 "Now may the God of peace, who through the blood of the eternal covenant brought back from the dead our Lord Jesus, that great Shepherd of the sheep, equip you with everything good for doing his will, and may he work in us what is pleasing to him, through Jesus Christ, to whom be glory forever and ever. Amen." —NIV

Restored Salvation

The feeling where you become numb to the one that saved you and knew you before life had begun
You start to wonder if this is it or if God wants you to be happy
If the journey is made up in your head or if you're stalling your calling
And no matter how hard you try to breathe and stand, you know you're falling
Am I spiritually suffocating?
When God first saved you, you felt like your soul was levitating
Meditating on His word daily
Now you've become lukewarm lazy
Your mind is all spacey
And everyone around you, including life itself, seems hazy
And you tell yourself maybe you'll muster up the energy to pray tomorrow or today
Sweat on your face, feeling like a disgrace
Tears all over your pillowcase
Longing to rest in Him, but you feel like you failed His tests
Your sin crept in, and at the moment, you thought it was the best choice
What's there left to rejoice in
My patience is wearing thin
I'm bleeding within
So God restore to me
The joy of my salvation
I need hope now
I don't want to live empty
I need your grace
Oh, listen to my cry as I fall on my face

Prostrated before you
For against you only have I sinned
Forgive me for being stagnant
Though my soul is dull, please don't null your promise
For you are my portion
I know this distortion won't last
Don't cast me from your presence, oh God
Could you open my eyes once again so I can see?
I've allowed the world to get ahold of me
Now I long to behold your face once again
Have mercy on me, my God
As your rod draws me in
May it comfort me
No more being in a tailspin
I will be quick to heed and obey
I'm tired of the delay
I've waited night and day
I don't want to live just to be okay
But may my spirit overflow with joy as I do your will
Come once again and tell me to be still
I weep tears of repentance
Seek this lost sheep
Lest she falls asleep
And be as one among the dead.

Psalm 51:12 "Restore to me the joy of your salvation, and make me willing to obey you. —NLT

Psalm 119:176 "I have strayed like a lost sheep. Seek your servant, for I have not forgotten your commands" —NIV

Eternal Life

Made in your image
In your likeness
Spirit, soul, and flesh
Called to life with your spirit kiss
No longer knowing death
Out of the dust, we came
And to the dust, we shall return
My life is a mist
Here today and gone tomorrow
It sounds like empty bliss
But I know I won't be left amiss
You rose from the grave
Death has been conquered, defeated
Now you're seated
At the right hand of the one
Who knew me before my life even begun
You have my heart
Now I'm a part of your kingdom
Heaven bound
With you is where I want to be forever found.

Genesis 1:27 So God created human beings in his own image. In the image of God he created them; male and female, he created them. —NLT

Genesis 2:7 Then the LORD God formed a man from the dust of the ground and breathed into his nostrils the breath of life, and the man became a living being." —NIV.

1 Corinthians 15: "Where, O death, is your victory? Where, O death, is your sting?" —NIV

Mark 16:19: "So then, when the Lord Jesus had spoken to them, He was received up into heaven and sat down at the right hand of God." —NASB

Victory from Resisting Temptation

(One of the best feelings is knowing that you've said no to sin when you could of gave in.. a poem about experiencing joy in the midst of overcoming)
God, you're so faithful
You say resist the devil, and he will flee
This I did indeed
I laugh with glee
You've gently tilted up my chin
You're the victory within
You're shaking off these rough edges
My body was about to give in to sin
But the enemy did not win
People, when you're tempted, listen to Him
To that still small voice of the Holy Spirit within
The Lord will fight your battles when you call upon His name
Come under the blood
You who the Father so loves
To the one who can shield you
To the one who will keep you
Honor and glory and power to His name
To the lamb who was slain
The mane, the lion of Judah
Forever and ever
Amen

James 4:7 "Submit yourselves, then, to God. Resist the devil, and he will flee from you." —NIV.

1 Corinthians "No temptation has overtaken you except what is common to mankind. And God is faithful; he will not let you be tempted beyond what you can bear. But when you are tempted, he will also provide a way out so that you can endure it. —NIV

Fight to the Light

Cling to the light, they say
Fight to it
You shine so brightly
I'm on my knees begging, please
Change my insides before I come to ruin
Get rid of this disease
That's in my mind
And bring me ease
In you
Rid me of this affliction of addiction
Make me long for only you
Cause nothing else to satisfy
Keep me tue
All those empty worldly lies
Those ugly soul ties
The struggle is real
Not to reach for that pill
I get high from the thrill
But I know it'll just make me ill
Do fill this vessel with your truth
Remember not my sins from my youth
Self-control is what I need
Don't let me sit alone out here to bleed
It just feels so hard to breathe
I hear you saying, "follow my lead."
I just want to swallow another one
Then I promise I'll be done
But it's just more lies
It'll never end
Who am I to pretend
Get my head together
I can't offend

Those around me
The beautiful people
The gifts you've given me
I can't do it, but I want to
I'll let it fill me
Then it'll kill me I'll
leave them all behind
Why am I still blind?
I've tried to walk in your ways, oh Lord
But these trials are putting me to shame
And help me not to blame you
Surround me with your ministering crew of angels
Only you can help me to be the person you created me
to be
So I choose you to help me stay clean
I lean not on my own understanding
But everything that you mean
Here comes your son
Saving me
Only you understand
I know you have a plan
You're now breaking though
I know it's you
Teaching me how to stay true
Making me new, making me new.

1 John 4:4 "But you belong to God, my dear children. You
have already won a victory over those people, because the
Spirit who lives in you is greater than the spirit who lives
in the world." —NLT.

1 Peter 5:6-8 "Humble yourselves, therefore, under God's mighty hand, that he may lift you up in due time. Cast all your anxiety on him because he cares for you. Be alert and of sober mind. Your enemy the devil prowls around like a roaring lion looking for someone to devour." —NIV.

Delightful Servant

Beautiful vessel
It's time to let me bring all the walls down
Don't frown; I'm making your crown more adorning
Your heart has been through some pain
But I'm here to drain away the harrow
And wash away your sorrows
I've seen you cry on your pillow every night in the past
My eye has always been on you
You have a lot to give
But some fear still holds you back
It's okay
Remember, pain and love go together
I'm breaking your heart to feed the flocks
Daughters will sit at your feet and listen
They will weep and cling unto you
For I am making you an example
My love will be seen through your eyes
As you extend your time
With joy, you'll walk with your head held
high And won't pass them by Look!
I am doing a new thing in you
Can you not perceive it?
Do you not hear it?
Come close and listen.
Open up your heart and come under my full submission
Loving others is your mission
I will whisper a morsel of truth in your Spirit
That you will proclaim to the masses so they can hear it
They will come near you, my dear
So be of good cheer
I am here with you doing this.

John 13:34 "So now I am giving you a new commandment: Love each other. Just as I have loved you, you should love each other." —NLT.

Restore

Where's that on-fire girl that I knew?
She walked away today.
With all of her hope
She's trying
Holding on with a loose grip
It started off tight but
The light within is growing dim
She was knocking on the door, and there was no
response Why, God, do you not respond when I knock?
I can't breathe, sweat breaking out; I'm in need
Where's the savior that unlocked my heart?
The one who knew me from the start
He said we'd never be apart So did
you depart my God?
My savior and my friend?
I feel further from Him now than ever
Restore God
Restore hope, my God
They have shamed me
They have filled me with misery
My lips ache and tremble
I long to sing your praises once again Most High
But the words crack out
Could you fill me with joy once again?
The joy I have in your name
Your name is what I cling to
Your name remains in me
They despise me, God
My hope is nearly cut off
My reputation is gone
I am made low
Those I once knew won't even greet me in public

They treat me like an enemy
The people I once worshiped with
It pains me to talk about it
I'm broken
It hurts
The memories piercing back at me
Where's the girl I knew?
The girl I knew?
Help me, my God
Could you remind me?
Remind me once again
And restore once more.

Psalm 51:12 "Restore to me the joy of your salvation and grant me a willing spirit, to sustain me." —NIV.

Psalm 41:9 "Even my best friend, the one I trusted completely, the one who shared my food, has turned against me." —NLT

Daughters

(A poem written for the daughters of God.. you're lionesses made to roar)

Lionesses Arise
Comparison will try to be your demise
Don't look to the left or right
Look up to the master, your heart's delight
It doesn't matter what people think of you
Just let Him see you through
Arise and Roar
And in Him, you'll soar.

2 Corinthians 10:12- "Not that we dare to classify or compare ourselves with some of those who are commending themselves. But when they measure themselves by one another and compare themselves with one another, they are without understanding." —ESV.

Philippians 2:3 Do nothing from selfish ambition or conceit, but in humility count others more significant than yourselves. —ESV

John 2:23 "But Jesus would not entrust himself to them, for he knew all people.He did not need any testimony about mankind, for he knew what was in each person." —NIV

Psalms 46:5 "God is in the midst of her, she will not be moved; God will help her when morning dawns." —NASB.

Runaway

I'm undone
So undone
To the one
That won my heart
By the love, He shows me
And I
I'm lost for words
That you've chosen me
Oh God
You caress my face
You say, "it's never too late."
To enter into my grace
I'll bring you back even when you run
My seal is on you
You're my beloved
Oh, you're my beloved
You're mine.

Luke 15:24 "For this son of mine was dead and is alive again; he was lost and is found.' So they began to celebrate." —NIV

Mustard Seed

(Jesus said it takes having faith of a mustard seed to experience the miraculous. So what's stopping us? A poem about overcoming fear of the future and applying that seed of faith)

Fear of the future can feel so real God
I cry on the floor in the middle of the night
Asking God to take away this fright in my heart
On my own, I'm so weak
I can't do it, but He speaks softly to me and says, by His grace, I'll get through it.
The only person holding you back from your destiny is the person reflecting back at you in the mirror.
How can I make this any clearer
I had to learn the hard way
If you want something you can't stay in the same place
Get up, child, run your race
In this life, it's hard not to lose face
So chin up, concentrate
No longer taking any second for granted
God gives us the vision
Now it's up to us to make it our mission
To use wisdom and to apply the work of our hands
Read these words and understand
Partner with the Holy Ghost who knows you most
Get with Him so you can win
Fear of man will try to bring you down
Will try to cheat you out of your heavenly crown
Don't allow anything to distort His plans
Turn your faith around
Stay strong; the enemy is always wrong
You have to push forward

Go towards what He put in your heart to long for
God will open the right door
Just trust in Him
Faith as a mustard seed.

2: Corinthians 12:9 "But he said to me, "My grace is sufficient for you, for my power is made perfect in weakness." Therefore I will boast all the more gladly about my weaknesses, so that Christ's power may rest on me." —NIV

Matthew 17:20 "You don't have enough faith," Jesus told them. "I tell you the truth, if you had faith even as small as a mustard seed, you could say to this mountain, 'Move from here to there,' and it would move. Nothing would be impossible." —NLT

1 Timothy 4:14 "Do not neglect the spiritual gift within you, which was bestowed on you through prophetic utterance with the laying on of hands by the presbytery." —NASB 1995

Obey the Call

I've come to the end of my wits
What's the point of even trying
No more denying your timing
I'm listening to your call
I know I no longer can stall
Lord, remove these walls
What is your will for my life?
How come no one told me what the true cost is like?
I guess I have to consider all these heartaches as lost
Giving up relationships that aren't of you
Sometimes I feel like my heart is being pierced though
But there are you
Telling me to hang on and to be strong and that you're
going to make this all-new
Sometimes I can't front I feel so sad.
Having to walk in purity, watching all these married
people around me
Please explain to me, God, how rejection is equaling
protection right now?
Cause I don't get it
My life is yours
My body is yours
In complete submission, I give myself to the call
No longer will I stall
You lift me each time I fall
Poured out like water
My heart within me is weak
You say blessed are the meek, for they will inherit the
earth
To the world, I have no worth
I feel like nothing
But in you, I am everything

Your truth speaks a better word
My insides groan
Outwardly I moan
Get me out of this miry pit!
When will you set me on fire again?
The first love we had, I crave
Tears drench my face
My spirit is hungry for you
All this for you, God
Show me you're here and that it will all be worth it
That your Son deserves it
For I am lowly and hurting
I don't know what the future holds or where to go
Thinking ahead gives my heart anxiety
Show me my steps God and where to start
Direct my path
For you have saved me from your wrath.

Proverbs 3:5 "Trust in the Lord with all your heart and lean not on your own understanding; in all your ways submit to him, and he will make your paths straight."—NIV

Matthew 5:5 "Blessed are the meek, for they will inherit the earth." —NIV

"Romans 5:9 "Since we have now been justified by his blood, how much more shall we be saved from God's wrath through him!" —NIV

Wrestle For Purity

(A poem written while struggling with purity)

The emptiness kicks in again
Where are you tonight?
In this dark hour
The shadows seem so bright
Where is your light?
That casts out the lies
I've tried
But I don't want to anymore
How to trust
When it's so easy to lust
After the world
I want you
But you have to pull me through
Please don't forsake me
The loneliness kills
Are you protecting me?
Or am I just unlucky
I say I don't need it
I don't want it
But I do
"You're so young," they say
Wow, tell me something I don't know
It's not what I want to hear
Whisper something else in my ear
Just trying to follow God in the 21st century
In a western world
Could you help me, Jesus?
To stay pure
And not to lure

After everything else
That isn't of You
Help me to remain faithful.

1 Corinthians 10:13 "No temptation has overtaken you except what is common to mankind. And God is faithful; he will not let you be tempted beyond what you can bear. But when you are tempted, he will also provide a way out so that you can endure it." —NIV

1 Corinthians 6:15-20 "Do you not know that your bodies are parts of Christ?
Shall I then take away the parts of Christ and make them parts of a prostitute? Far from it! Or do you not know that the one who joins himself to a prostitute is one body with her? For He says, "The two shall become one flesh." But the one who joins himself to the Lord is one spirit with Him. Flee sexual immorality. Every other sin that a person commits is outside the body, but the sexually immoral person sins against his own body. Or do you not know that your body is a temple of the Holy Spirit within you, whom you have from God, and that you are not your own? For you have been bought for a price: therefore glorify God in your body."
—NASB

Like Christ

I want to be an imitator of my creator
He's my number one savior
Always on my radar
Come Jesus have your way
Display your greatness today
Fire fall down, I pray
We want your glory in full blast
And this time, we want it to last
Lord, please bring healing and salvation fast
Remove the stains of our past
The sins that try to rise up
When will we walk it out?
Open our homes
Open our hearts, God
That's when revival will break out
Without a doubt
The outside will see us and will desire the unity we carry
Until we do, then revival tarries
Kill the selfishness, the excuses
We want to go back to that early church
It's biblical
It's truth
Hold hands, prophecy
Wait for the spirit, not man made lies
In the upper room, seek the Holy Ghost
No more playing church
What happened to apostles like Paul's
Going outside the four walls
Time to go out and seek the lost
And counting the cost.

Luke 14:28 "For which of you, desiring to build a tower, does not first sit down and count the cost, whether he has enough to complete it?" —ESV

1 Corinthians 11:1 "And you should imitate me, just as I imitate Christ." —NLT Luke 19:10 "For the Son of Man came to seek and save those who are lost." —NLT

Fight for Purity

I'm looking around to see if you're there God, do you even care?
I toss and turn
Oh, how I yearn for your spirit to revive me
Please teach me how to discern
How to learn to hear your voice
Empower me by your spirit to have the choice to choose you over this noise

As I lie alone in bed
I think, "Is this it? Is this the life I dread?"
You smile and act funny when they're around.
And drown yourself in your own space, asking God to help you not lose faith
You think you're content, but the loneliness takes place, and you wonder how you got here again
You're lonely
Lonely
And you know a one-night stand won't satisfy
You need to choose Jesus and not live in these empty lies
But your flesh wants to gratify, wants to feel alive
You think having another person there will repair the issues you have inside
But what you don't realize is that if you dive into that, you'll build up those soul ties
You're reasoning with yourself in your mind, "what if I do it once"?
But you know if you give in, you can't go back and rewind
So you cry out to God so the enemy won't rob you of your innocence
Asking Him to save you from your own destruction
God, get me out of this dungeon!

Allow your words to pierce me.
Your word is better than this desire
I am yours, my God
My body belongs to you
This vessel you breathed to life
Is all yours
My spirit is a willing temple
You are greater than the fight inside
Come with your spirit and power
Breath of God, revive me in this hour.

Hebrews 4:12 "For the word of God is alive and active. Sharper than any double-edged sword, it penetrates even to dividing soul and spirit, joints and marrow; it judges the thoughts and attitudes of the heart." —NIV.

John 16:8 "When he comes, he will prove the world to be in the wrong about sin and righteousness and judgment" —NIV.

Wrestle with Condemnation

My heart is distressed
How often will you put me to the test?
I need to take a breath and digress
It's time for me to get this off of my chest
God, you alone is whom I want to serve
But so many times, I fail and feel like I don't deserve
Your sacrifice and your advice
From your Holy Word
Sometimes I feel like I'm going absurd
I fall every day
And I hate myself after it
My soul is in disarray
Please help me to see myself as you do
Could you give me the grace to pull through?
I'm your child that makes mistakes
But doesn't fall far from your face
A child that messes up
But to you, she's always enough
A child that doesn't always make the best decisions
But you step in with your Holy Spirit incision
He gives me the conviction
Shows me that I'm fully forgiven
And with you, life is worth living
When I feel too ashamed to run back to you
And I feel the need to make myself feel blamed
When my heart is feeling so pained
Please show me the entire inheritance that I have gained
In Christ Jesus
Cause you paid the price
For my life.

Romans 8:1-2 "Therefore, there is now no condemnation for those who are in Christ Jesus, because through Christ Jesus the law of the Spirit who gives life has set you free from the law of sin and death." —NIV

Romans 8:26 "Likewise the Spirit helps us in our weakness. For we do not know what to pray for as we ought, but the Spirit himself intercedes for us with groanings too deep for words." —ESV

Give Me Hope

I know the thoughts of suicide and not wanting to be alive
Believe me; I thought if I buried my feelings deep within,
they would go away
Feeling like I'm underwater
Lifeless as I walk the earth
Your dreams feel blurred, and life isn't what it seems
I wouldn't have deemed I would have felt so low
It feels like my soul took a blow
But you feel a tickle of hope in your veins, regardless of
the pains that ache within you.
Trying to mend the broken pieces.
The colors look dark, and I can't find the spark of faith
How did Noah feel on that arc?
On this journey of staying clean but in some moments, I
want to scream.
I see the people around me on the subway
Faces are dreams that lost their expiration dates
Gloomy, tired, restless souls
Striving till their old
Tell me that there's more to life than this
I felt my dreams had passed their expiration date
Feeling like it's too late Am I the one at fault?
The voices in my head say to lock my aspirations in a vault
They tell me to stop dreaming

Not really here now, living in a mental torture

I know I must sit at your feet and bow but
It seems I've forgotten to dwell in your presence now.

The room is dimly lighted, and I'm crawled up, sitting in
the corner

Speechless
My tears are words screaming louder to the heavens
I've come to the end of my wits
I shout out for salvation
A weak cry rises up
It surfaces from the core of my deep as it bubbles up
while I weep.
You meet me where I am
You swoop me away
Wrapped in your arms, this is the place I want to stay
And this poem becomes about hope now
Light came into me
Now I know that everything will be okay
I have a purpose; it's not too late
I'm fully alive and breathing
And your voice is heeding to my hunger cries
Your love is echoing inside as it dispels the lies
My God is the living water I'm drinking
Refreshing the soul, refreshing the depths of my being
All I had to do was come and be still
And know that you're God
So be still, oh my soul
Be still and quiet within me
The Lord will revive vision
He will restore oh my soul
Put your trust in Him alone
He gives life and hope
Come and receive my soul
From the fountains of life
The Lord is His name
The Lord will radiate this dark night
So no more fright, oh my soul
As He becomes your heart's delight.

Psalm 42:5 "Why, my soul, are you downcast? Why so disturbed within me? Put your hope in God, for I will yet praise him, my Savior and my God." —NIV

Psalm 46:10 "He says, "Be still, and know that I am God; I will be exalted among the nations, I will be exalted in the earth." —NIV

Psalm 37:4 "Delight yourself in the LORD, and he will give you the desires of your heart." —ESV

Proverbs 3:5-6 "Trust in the Lord with all your heart; do not depend on your own understanding. Seek his will in all you do, and he will show you which path to take." —NLT

Descend

Her heart has been broken
Torn in two
Lord show her all of those promises
The ones you have spoken to in the quiet of her soul
There's a deep fight within her that needs to be awoken
But her faith has been shaken
The enemy has taken away her joy
Jerking her around like a toy
She gave in to the lie
She longer wants to try
A cry as she looks up to the sky
Wondering why you've allowed all this pain
Playing the blame game again
My God, My God
Why hast thou forsaken me?
I wish you would have taken me
Up to your throne, into your home
Oh Lord
I want you, God
I want to feel you
I want to know you
And the depths of you
Let the fire of your passion ignite in my veins
Break these chains
Begin to start a new thing in me
Till it's only you that I see
I want to know all of you, Lord God almighty
That is your name
You're the Lord
You're Holy
You're worthy
My thoughts have been foolish

Forgive my rebellion
Have mercy on me, my king
Fill me with your Spirit and truth
May it be the satisfaction of my soul
I desire this
Make me new
Bring the cravings of the flesh to death
Till only you remain
I don't want to be the same anymore
For I am an expression of your love
So Holy Spirit, please come
And descend on me like a dove.

Romans 8:26 "Likewise the Spirit helps us in our weakness. For we do not know what to pray for as we ought, but the Spirit himself intercedes for us with groanings too deep for words." —ESV

Refresh Lord

All this pain I feel on the inside.
I thought you would take it all away and make me feel
fully alive
My flesh and my spirit are fighting a war
The violence within me is great
The temptation to self-destruct and numb myself is
knocking
Heaviness, where did you come from?
Why am I this way?
I feel like no one understands
God, please open up your hands
Please show me your plans, help me
I am an outcast
God, how long will these feelings last?
I want to receive your freedom
Breath of God, breathe
Why do I want to self-medicate?
Instead of allowing your spirit to operate within me?
I feel unworthy
Worthless indeed
I feel like I deserve the hard way
What is wrong with me, Yahweh?
This is how I feel today
Waking up, sexual thoughts flood my mind
All the past trauma and pain hit me like a rewind
I thought I was doing fine, but it seems I was blind to this
sudden attack
Fear holds me back
It is why I lack to go deeper
Restless I am
Darkness encamps my mind like a thick cloud
My soul cries aloud

I want to feel loved
I want to feel known
I want to scream
I'm feeling a million different things
I want the void to be filled
My flesh wants to indulge in sin
But is it worth it?
No …
You've placed me in a good place
In your bosom, I am safe
So help me to stay pure
And not to lure after worthless things
I want to make you proud
Let laughter arise up within me
Holy Ghost, burn the terrible thoughts away
I only want you to stay
Don't let this sheep go astray
Help me to stay in a place of clarity
God be my gravity!
I'm making a choice
To come close and hear your voice
To rise above the noise
So please speak to me now
I sit here at your feet and bow.

2 Corinthians 10:5-6 "We demolish arguments and every
pretension that sets itself up against the knowledge
of God, and we take captive every thought to make it
obedient to Christ. And we will be ready to punish every
act of disobedience, once your obedience is complete."
—NIV.

Hebrews 4:12 "For the word of God is alive and active. Sharper than any double-edged sword, it penetrates even to dividing soul and spirit, joints and marrow; it judges the thoughts and attitudes of the heart." —NIV.

His Righteousness

Isaiah 61:10 reads,

"I delight greatly in the Lord; my soul rejoices in my God. For he has clothed me with garments of salvation and arrayed me in a robe of his righteousness, as a bridegroom adorns his head like a priest, and as a bride adorns herself with her jewels" —NIV

Rejoice greatly in the Lord God almighty.
Allow your soul to praise Him.
It was created to praise Him, to be glad in Him, to have joy in Him!
That is your portion! Your soul WILL REJOICE IN HIM!
He clothes us with His salvation.
He clothes us and covers us with the power of His blood.
He destroys the chains.
He breaks the yoke of the oppressor.
With His rod and staff, He crushes the seemingly unbreakable shackles.

The robe of this righteousness encircles you.
The robe of His righteousness is interwoven in and through you.
Just as a bridegroom covers his head with his turban
And as a bride on her wedding day covers herself in intricate, beautiful jewelry.
So how much more glorious are His garments on you, matchless and magnificent?
The best part is.. He FREELY gives them to us.

You are the righteousness of God in Christ Jesus.

2 Corinthians 5:21 "God made him who had no sin to be sin for us, so that in him we might become the righteousness of God" —NIV

Creators Craft

The hand of the Creator
Which hath made me
The hand of the Creator
In which I am blessed
You saved me
You saved me!
Jesus, I love you
Jesus, I love you!
Your love is endless
Like the ocean
It runs deep
I feel you in my bones
You're all around me, God
I feel you in the air
With every breath that I take
There's no other
Lord, there's only you
You created all
My savior
In your son, I am set free
By His blood, I am saved
Oh so loved
I can't think of anything better
Sacrificed, tormented, and mocked
But you kept going by His command
Your journey to the cross saved man
Now you're beside Him at the throne
In your kingdom is someday where I hope to be
Oh God, what you do to me.

Hebrews 12:2 "fixing our eyes on Jesus, the author, and perfecter of faith, who for the joy set before Him endured the cross, despising the shame, and has sat down at the right hand of the throne of God." —NASB 1995

Isaiah 64:8 "Yet you, LORD, are our Father. We are the clay, you are the potter; we are all the work of your hand." —NIV.

Psalm 8:3-5 "When I consider your heavens, the work of your fingers, the moon and the stars, which you have set in place, what is mankind that you are mindful of them, human beings that you care for them"? —NIV

Behind the Veil

There's pain behind your eyes
You look in the mirror and wonder why
"Why do I feel this way?"
Life is so sad
We all die
Life is summed up in heartfelt memories
They carry us in flashbacks
Generations pass, and the cycle begins again
We're here for a short while
And soon, generations after us forget we existed
Who remembers us but the Lord?
Whom are we living for but Him?
We make our mark on this land for His name
Nothing else counts
Nothing else will ever amount
And nothing else matters
Worldly dreams get shattered
Life is meaningless
Pointless without Him
For our mortal bodies see decay
Only He is the true way
Turn to Him today
Listen and obey
Can money buy the soul?
Or can it purchase eternal life?
Before He came, I picked up that knife
I wanted to end my pain
But I couldn't help and listen to Him when He called my
name
Life is sad and empty without God
The enemy goes around and tries to rob the creation of
this truth

The culture has bowed to the schemes of tv screens and luxury living
Entrapped by the media and news, it's all a ruse
We're feeding into our fears and idolizing the distractions around us
They're false ideas of happiness
None of us are truly happy
Never having peace
Never putting our hearts at ease
We're all broken on the inside
Screaming for the truth that lies in front of our eyes
But we push Him away
The narrow road is too hard, we say
Our minds go into disarray
We fill the void with temporary comforts
Binge watching, dating apps, jumping from relationship to relationship, drug addictions, and alcohol afflictions
We are all born with a knowledge of God, but there's a difference between knowing He's there and obeying His word.
Not everyone who simply believes is His child
Don't be deceived like Eve
Repent because He won't relent on His end-time plans
While there is still time, He says, "become mine."
It's your choice, life or death
So choose life
While there's still breath.

"Yet you do not know what your life will be like tomorrow. For you are just a vapor that appears for a little while, and then vanishes away." James 4:14 —NASB

Psalm 103:14"For he knows our frame; he remembers that we are dust." —ESV

Romans 1:20 "For since the creation of the world His invisible attributes, His eternal power and divine nature, have been clearly seen, being understood through what has been made, so that they are without excuse." —NASB 1995

Bondservant of Christ

Seal me with this love
Enrich it in my heart
Streaming through my veins
You're life
You're living
I'm a walking expression of your love
Your spirit kiss brought me to life
Angels sing
Great is the lamb who overcame
Master of the heavens
You reign
And He sends his rain on the wicked and good
He does as He pleases
All belongs to him
Father, as I walk, I see things through your eyes
Feel the empty lives around me and hear their cries
I feel the yearning for you to help
Father, my soul sees clearly now
You are alive with me in my spirit
The fire of your love has given me discernment
I didn't have to earn it
Oh, to learn the joy of the Lord
Now what can I do, oh Lord
Please, my God, save them
There are too many that still need to know your name
I feel like I can do so much more
Oh, Jesus, I want you to tell me what to do
Guide my mind and my heart
Show me where to start
Allow me to be your soldier on earth
To live and serve you as you command As I long to walk
according to your plan.

1 Corinthians 7:22 "For he who was called in the Lord as a bondservant is a freedman of the Lord. Likewise he who was free when called is a bondservant of Christ." —ESV.

1 Corinthians 6:19-20 "Do you not know that your bodies are temples of the Holy Spirit, who is in you, whom you have received from God? You are not your own; you were bought at a price. Therefore honor God with your bodies." —NIV.

Faith

God, I've got faith
As small as a mustard seed
Could you make it grow?
Cause this season feels so dull
And I
I can't find the words
You say tears are intercession
Come, count and collect them in your bottle
I'm losing sight of reality
Eyes squinting, where are you now?
I'm waiting, waiting
Where are the words?
The words..
A sigh as I look up to the heavens
You're in between my thoughts
The lines have fallen
I'm waiting, waiting …
Love of the Father comes pouring out …
Pour out on me now …

Matthew 17:20 "He replied, "Because you have so little faith. Truly I tell you, if you have faith as small as a mustard seed, you can say to this mountain, 'Move from here to there,' and it will move. Nothing will be impossible for you." —NIV

Psalm 16:5-6 "Lord, you alone are my portion and my cup; you make my lot secure. The boundary lines have fallen for me in pleasant places; surely I have a delightful inheritance." —NIV

Psalm 56:8 "You have taken account of my miseries; Put my tears in Your bottle. Are they not in Your book?" —NASB

Purify

Refine your bride
Cause if I'm not living for you, then I'm living a lie
Like silver in the fire
Test me like gold
Purify this vessel
I want to walk wholeheartedly in your ways
Before I get put down in the grave
Teach me to number my days
Fill my spirit with the wonders of your love
You're the lover of my soul
My first love
I cry out for you
I'm in love with you
My heart burns daily for more of you
You're All I need
All I want
We are one
You in me
Father, Spirit, and Son
Let's go away
With you is where I want to stay forever.

Zechariah 13:9 "I will bring that group through the fire and make them pure. I will refine them like silver and purify them like gold. They will call on my name, and I will answer them. I will say, 'These are my people,' and they will say, 'The LORD is our God." —NLT.

No other Like You

Your name makes the mountains shake
Your voice can make the earthquake
You break the curse of sin and make my soul awake
You breathe new life within
Jesus, you are power
Full of majesty and wonder
Glorious in splendor
You render the heavens
No other name is like yours
Oh, just the name
Heals
Oh, just the name
Saves
Jesus
Jesus Christ
The living hope of the nations
Break
Break open in the atmosphere
Break
Break open prison doors
Lord I implore
Please show us what you have in store
Oh, we need so much more of who you are
We are empty vessels in need of you to fill us up
Like an empty cup we are, fill us up to overflow in your
presence
Weak we come, and humbly we receive
Poor in spirit, blessed are we
And in the presence of my enemies, you prepare a table
before me
Their voices are silenced cause it is the great king who
sits next to me

You rescue and save
You deliver me from the grave!
I will forever rave about your great name.

Psalm 51:17 "The sacrifice you desire is a broken spirit. You will not reject a broken and repentant heart, O God." —NLT.

Psalm 23:5 "You prepare a table before me in the presence of my enemies. You anoint my head with oil; my cup overflows." —NIV.

Praises

Thunder you heavens
Shout out for joy
Salivation has come
Love has made a way
Shout for joy, all you elders
Sing praises all you angels
Death has been conquered
The grave destroyed
Defeated
Shine a rainbow
Show your beauty
Be exalted blessed one
Look
The fierce and mighty Lion of Judah arises
He is coming and roars against evil
The king will rule with an iron fist
Justice, he will declare to the broken hearted
To the needy, he will feed
No one will ever hunger nor thirst again
With His own hands, he will wipe away the tears of the
righteous
The new Jerusalem is coming down from His dwelling
The Lord is the light of the temple
Endure all you people!
Endure till the end all you who fear The Lord!
For great is your reward.
Great is your crown that he will place on your head
We will reign with Him and take charge
We are the sons and daughters
Heirs to the holy throne
God declares, "I am making all things new."
He is coming

He is coming soon
Our beloved bridegroom.

Revelation 4:10-11 "The twenty-four elders fall down before him who sits on the throne and worship him who lives for ever and ever. They lay their crowns before the throne and say: "You are worthy, our Lord and God, to receive glory and honor and power, for you created all things, and by your will they were created and have their being." —NIV.

Revelation 5:5 "Then one of the elders said to me, "Do not weep! See, the Lion of the tribe of Judah, the Root of David, has triumphed. He is able to open the scroll and its seven seals." —NIV.

Revelation 2:26-28 "To the one who is victorious and does my will to the end, I will give authority over the nations—that one 'will rule them with an iron scepter and will dash them to pieces like pottery'—just as I have received authority from my Father. I will also give that one the morning star." —NIV.

Revelation 7 "Never again will they hunger; never again will they thirst. The sun will not beat down on them,' nor any scorching heat." —NIV.

Revelation 21:4 "He will wipe every tear from their eyes. There will be no more death or mourning or crying or pain, for the old order of things has passed away." —NIV.

Revelation 21:3 "The city does not need the sun or the moon to shine on it, for the glory of God gives it light, and the Lamb is its lamp." —NIV

Matthew 24:13 "But the one who endures to the end will be saved." —NLT

Lovesick Girl

Nothing compares to what is between us God
You dwell within the chambers of my soul
This love is unbreakable
Unshakeable
Nothing can sweep it away
I linger to you, God
You have your finger on my life
Don't let me go, I pray
In the night, I toss and turn
My heart yearns for Him
I feel your love surrounding me
How is it that you love me so?
I am beautiful in your eyes, yes, lovely and perfect
There is no imperfection in me to you
All I have is yours, and I surrender myself entirely to you
When will you come down and rescue me?
When will I be at home with you?
Your hand was always with me; I know that now.
Though darkness surrounded me for years, you were
always there
You always pursued me, and you continue to do so
What kind of love is this?
I have fallen for you.
No longer will I fight it
I give into your love; I give in.

Song of Songs 3:1 "All night long on my bed
I looked for the one my heart loves;
I looked for him but did not find him. —NIV

Dialogue with God

Me: God, the struggle to stop the thoughts in my head
feels like it just won't end
I leave them unsaid; will I bring them with me till I'm
dead?
Too ashamed to announce them all Will it become my
downfall?
I shouldn't feel this way, should I?
Especially about you
How do you see me? How do you love me?
Get rid of this depression
My mind is in a mental oppression
I need hope; they accuse me and surround me
God, speak to me, give me direction!

The Counselor:
"I see you, my child
Your lost passions become my fight

Me: Lord, you're my soul's delight!

The Counselor: "Be still and know that you can rest in me
Depend on me
When I'm with you, I'm not playing pretend
I don't want any second with you to end
Each breath counts
And nothing in this world cant amount
To how uniquely I love you
Your soul is my work of art
And when you depart from this earth
It's me you'll forever be with

Me: Lord, my worth is in you!

Oh, you're so faithful and true
My soul comes awake when you speak!
Hope was bleak, and I didn't think my weak love would reach you
But you've spoken, and my heart has awoken to your love
Holy Ghost falls on me like a dove Oh, awaken love!
From the depths of my soul!
My faithful King put a ring on me
A sealed promise
I love you, Lord my strength
You have given me joy
You've seen how much I've cried and have revived me
Each droplet was not wasted
I have tasted your goodness
I love you; I love you!
My length of days will be measured by the joy of the Lord
His strength in me is all I need
I will testify, and the world will see
Christ in me
The hope of glory
The author of my story.

Psalm 24:8-10 "Who is the King of glory? The Lord strong and mighty, The Lord mighty in battle. Lift up your heads, you gates, And lift them up, you ancient doors, That the King of glory may come in! Who is this King of glory? The Lord of armies, He is the King of glory." —NASB.

His Beloved Bride:

Your fingers painted the stars
Your hands opened the earth
My name inscribed on your palms
You have put your seal upon my heart
Written in your book of life
What can man do to me?
Revived by your story
Amazed by your glory
Redeemer, you have opened me up
Like a beautiful flower
I was closed and had no root
But you planted me and caused me to spring forth
I now have truth and meaning
I am the apple of your eye
I will come away with you
Let's run together into the light of day

"See, I have engraved you on the palms of my hands; your walls are ever before me."- Isaiah 49:16 —NIV.

Psalm 19:1 "For the director of music. A psalm of David. The heavens declare the glory of God; the skies proclaim the work of his hands." —NIV.

The Beloveds Response:

Come, my beloved
Come away with me
Oh, how beautiful you are
Rose of Sharon says
I am taking you by the hand and holding it in mine
There is no flaw in you
No stain, no blemish
I have washed you
My glory shines in you
You are a lamp
There is no darkness in you
I am the bright and morning star
The Root of Jesse
Allow me to love on you so you can be more like me
No harm will overtake you, my beloved
I am covering you with my wings
My arm is strong
I, the Lord, am a mighty warrior
Defending those I love
Crushing the wicked and humbling the proud in heart.

Song of Songs 4:7 "You are altogether beautiful, my darling; there is no flaw in you." —NIV

Psalm 91:4 "He will cover you with his feathers, and under his wings, you will find refuge; his faithfulness will be your shield and rampart." —NIV

In Need

I don't want to sleep, my beloved
I don't want to miss a moment with you
How I long for your kisses
Sweeter than honey
My heart is set on you
Your love echoes from the deepest part of my soul
Invade my dreams tonight so that I can stay with you
Hold me as I rest away
Be the first one I hear and see at every waking moment
I never want to be apart from you
You said, "never will I leave you."
You're a keeper of your word.
You never lie
Am I out of my mind?
No, just in love
With the one
Who had formed me and holds my heart
You're my deepest desire
My greatest treasure
So gentle and precious
I'm sinking into your arms
Your ways are perfect
Your ways are so good
Your path is gold
I don't care what the world thinks
I want more of you, Abba
Lead me to the rock that is higher than I.

Psalm 61:2 "From the ends of the earth I call to you, I call as my heart grows faint; lead me to the rock that is higher than I." —NIV.

Psalm 119:105 "Your word is a lamp to my feet and a light to my path. —ESV

Genesis 15:1 "After this, the word of the LORD came to Abram in a vision: "Do not be afraid, Abram. I am your shield, your very great reward." —NIV.

Beyond the Horizon

The light went through her heart that day
For the first time, she heard the good news
She now knew she could never depart from her beloved
"Oh, the lamb that was slain!" She exclaimed
"Before the foundations of the world!
Oh, the lamb that was slain!
Before the foundations of the world
Oh, the sweet mystery
Christ in me!"
Amazed, she pondered in her mind,
"Could this all be real?"

As she sat on the sand, she observed the sea beyond her.
As she looked on, her past memories began to resurface.
As they replayed in her head, she wished she could escape
the torment in her mind.

Not feeling worthy or qualified enough of the new birth
she had experienced, her heart was beating violently
within her.
"Remember.. She said to herself, "His blood speaks a
better word; His blood covers all who believe!"
The enemy tried to grip me in condemnation..
"No more agreement with his lies
Or allowing his little spies to cause my mind demise"..
She took deep breaths as she encouraged herself and
heard whispering echoes of truth now surrounding her,
giving her affirmation of her calling.
Revelations of her future were presented to her by angels
that walked by her side.
Since her birth, they were there, constantly aware,
strengthening her for these moments that were to come.

Deep treasure of life was taking place in her core being
The stirring was happening
She got up and walked down to the seashore to contemplate how this new life might transform her.

Every revelation He gave permeated her whole being
She did not want to withhold anything
She could not, even if she tried
All her deepest motives and intents were exposed
Every thought was known
The covenant was formed
A sealed inheritance A sacred bond took place The healing has begun.

As she gazed into the ocean, she thought of how perfectly the waves formed
How she felt like the water and her new beloved was each wave crashing over her, making her new with each covering and splash of life

The former things she knew were fading.
With each new step she took, she could feel her old ways escaping
She walked further onto the path
The sweet sounds of the voice of the one she longed to hear call out for her were growing louder.
"Should I walk towards it? What else can He possibly give me? Shall I walk closer to the voice that calls me by name?"

The different beams of light from the Sunkist sunset felt warm on her skin
Radiance was beaming all around her, and the path was shown for her to follow

The light illuminated on the ground, and she followed the way it created
Her thoughts of fear were deteriorating
Exhilarating bliss was filling her from the inside out
And every ounce of doubt was diminishing

As her fears were fading away, the windstorms around her started to cease
Her soft heart wanted to burst of freedom into the light path following the voice; her inner being craved for the second her eyes would meet the one calling her name from the distance
"I cannot go to sleep, she thought; I could lose it all"..
For a moment, she closed her eyes, and the sounds of His voice touched her core once again.
"Remind yourself again".. She said.. Remind..
"I'm covered by the blood; it's no foul
A scandal called grace saved me
Oh, amazing grace!
How sweet the sound!
He surrounds me with songs of DELIVERANCE
Wave after wave, Jesus' blood washes over me I am clean; I am free"..

The sweet whispers of "follow me" were all around her after she made declarations. The pure voice from a distance grew louder in volume when she paused her steps to think of memories from the past.
For moments, fear and condemnation gripped her and tried to weigh her down from this new life given. "I'll lose everything in this world," she thought..

"Could it be that I'm not worthy enough? I don't know if I can fully accept this new treasure of freedom". She then fell face down, discouraged as tears drenched the ground, and she could not muster the strength to go on. She had one more path to cross but was exhausted from the weighing down of her soul. Twisted thoughts of wanting to walk into the ocean and ending her path consumed her. Lies were now breathing into her, and the will to go on felt nearly impossible.

A nail-scarred hand caressed her face as she came to the end of herself. The voice she heard was more powerful than the sounds of a thousand rushing waterfalls. Holding her face to look directly into His eyes, then looking up to Heaven, He told his father in an authoritative yet gentle tone that she can now love much because she has been forgiven for much. The light behind her eyes is new; the love in her is true.

Oh, how the remembrance of her sin held her back from her God-given destiny!
It was all she could see
Every time she would rise in her calling
She kept on falling
Like a dark cloud encamped in her mind, she felt blind to the power of my blood.
Felt dirty once again, like she was covered in mud
The walls of Jericho felt like they would never come down
Like a prisoner encamped, she was bound
The enemies whispers were all around
The chains of depression enslaved her
The chains of condemnation gripped her
How the demons would not flee
And now, with the revelations of the love she receives from me
She will overflow to others

Looking into His compassionate eyes after hearing Him speak,, she whispered, "Beloved?"
"Beloved!?" She said twice with amazement." "Oh, Beloved, it's really you!" "It's you!" "Oh
Jesus, how much you love me!"

Smiling at her response, He asked her if she recalled when this all felt like a story. He questioned if she remembered the moments she sat alone gazing at the horizon, looking for where He might be.

"Yes, Lord!" She sang aloud. "I do!" "Now, as you hold me, I feel new rivers of water springing forth from my core being
Rushing, RUSHING, never-ending
The river of life! Rivers of living water!
I feel your compassion
You will not stop until I am like you
You relentlessly pursue me
You love me
You're not impatient!
The tender mercies of God
The tender mercies of the living God!
Kissing me
Tears well up in my eyes
I can't believe it; I can't believe it
Agreement with the enemy has been broken
I have used my mouth and have spoken
Your truths
I declared and confessed
Now you've taken care of the rest
My best doesn't count
Never did, never will amount
I can't make it up myself
I surrender. I surrender

Lord, I render my pride to you
I repent for not believing your blood was enough for my sins
I repent for not allowing you to take my pain within
It's beautiful what I feel
But oh, it's so real
Letting go and allowing you, Lord, to flow fully
Within all of me
The groanings are so deep!
I weep, I weep
Hold me as it fades away
Hold me as the old thinking decays
Hold me through the process
Hold me as I feel the vibrations of your love
Permeating my being
I'm ever seeing your kindness
Hold me as I'm letting go
You're exchanging something so beautiful for the old
It can't be put into language what is happening
The chains are destroyed
There's no longer that void
This is the beginning
Of something brand new
I feel like I'm winning
Oh in you
I feel different, brand new
Oh, you're the lamb that was slain!
Before the foundations of the world
Oh, the sweet mystery
Christ in me!"

Gently stroking her face, acknowledging that she was beginning to understand.
He told her that day after day; she used to wrestle with denying her flesh

Wrestled with not turning to the world or wanting to put
her body to death
Felt like she needed to self-punish and inflict
Keeping it a secret, fear of judgment from others
Felt so alone, like a failure for even thinking the thoughts
she did
Frustrated at herself for allowing her mind to go so far
Battling with not wanting to reside in the thoughts of
suicide
A constant strive to look to her to feel alive
Now she will fully abide in Him, The Most High.
Filled with joy as she looked into His eyes of love, she
broke out in song and sang,
"Oh, I finally understand! This was always your plan!
Before the foundations of the world!
Oh, I get it! Hear all of creation!
He thought this through!
Before there was even me and you!
He chose to cover His elect with His saving blood!
To all those who put their trust in Him!
In the covenant
His blood speaks a better word!
His blood covers a multitude of sins!
I'm covered by the blood.
DRENCHED in the cleansing!
I believe it fully, oh, no more heart-wrenching anguish!
His grace is sufficient!
His blood, His blood!
I can hear it!
I can see it
Taste it and feel it!
The tangible blood of Jesus!
Wave after wave, His blood washes over me!
I'm clean; I'm free!

He surrounds me with songs of DELIVERANCE He sings over me!

Wrapping His arms around her, He too then sang over her. He sang how beautiful it was now that her heart was open. He sang how she was His daughter and how her eyes have been opened to see the reality of Him. He then asked her to take His hand, and in doing so, He would show her what is far more extraordinary than what she had envisioned on this land. He told her to take His hand, and He will show her everything He has planned."
She felt safe as this nail-scarred hand caressed her face. He gently held her hand, and they walked on the sand together.
And from that moment on, she knew that she found true love and grace in His embrace.
For the living, God has forever stepped in and filled her space.

Revelation 13:8 "the Lamb slain from the foundation of the world."—BRG

Zephaniah 3:17 "The LORD your God in your midst, The Mighty One, will save; He will rejoice over you with gladness, He will quiet you with His love, He will rejoice over you with singing." —NKJV.

"I delight greatly in the LORD; My soul REJOICES in my God For he has clothed me with garments of salvation and arrayed me in a robe of HIS righteousness, as a bridegroom adorns his head like a priest, and as a bride adorns herself with her jewels." - Isaiah 61:10" —NIV.

Dear future child,

I've been anticipating your arrival
I've thought about you for awhile
I know you are not into the world yet but
I wonder the type of parent I can be
Thinking of the things I can do to make you happy
You see, growing up, my daddy didn't show me much love
I've felt a void
I was always annoyed when I saw relationships thriving in front of me
I'm not promising to be the perfect parent
But I promise always to be apparent
I understand being emotionally involved is more important than just seeming present.
These are the vows that I'm making to you now
On my knees, I bow to God and ask him to help me now
Oh, please, Lord, these are the words that I hope to promise to keep
Dear future child,
Whenever you're feeling weak, I'll be there to lift you high; I'll hug you tight and hold you close.
I'll let you know your worth, and I'll never let you go
I promise to be attentive
When you fall and have a boo-boo, I'll wipe the tears from your eyes and cherish every cry cause I know those moments won't be there forever.
I know these are just words, and I hope to keep them
I don't want to be the mom that you frown upon
You're my gift from God, and I know he gives crowns to the ones who overcome
He has won all the victories, and you're the most victorious one of them to me.
Dear future child

I promise to be patient
Never use harsh phrases
To never talk to you the way that my daddy used to talk
to me
I promise to cut the line of this generational curse
Cause the divine Lord has stepped into my life
He saved my soul and taught me what is right
Now I want to be a delight to you
It ends for good with past lines, and it starts anew with me
I'll try to be everything that God wants me to be for you
I hope to promise always to stay true
And if I struggle with a lack of being emotional for you,
I'll do whatever I can to make it right.
I know these inward wars don't go away overnight.
But whatever you suggest, I'll do my best to confess to God
I don't want this mess of my past family members to follow
Cause I can't lie, it all left me feeling hollow
And this pain feels so hard to swallow
If I'm breaking my vows and my patience is wearing thin,
I promise to get help.
I promise I'll fight to fix things.
This life is short, and I always want you to be in mine
You're a true treasure, a dime
The clock ticks and I know I won't be able to rewind and
fix any mistakes I may make, but you can always knock
on my door.
You have every area of my heart
There's not a piece of it that you aren't apart
The whole of it belongs to you
I'd give it all for you
The way Jesus laid down his life for you and I
I'll try my best to be the spitting image of Him to you in
front of your eyes.
Dear future child, dear future child..

Psalm 127:3 "Children are a gift from the Lord; they are a reward from him." —NLT

Ephesians 6:4 "Fathers, do not provoke your children to anger by the way you treat them. Rather, bring them up with the discipline and instruction that comes from the Lord." —NLT.

Godly Mothers

A smile that lights up the room
Your bridegroom has caused you to bloom
"You were born for such a time as this"
"I am calling you into the secret place of intercession and prayer."
In there, you will experience my pure bliss
"In my presence, you will cast all your cares."
A chosen mother
You open up your arms and your shoulders for others to lean on
You've given your time to those in need
You have been so generous to heed others
You have a gift for making those around you feel valued and loved
You're a pursuer of people, and His word
You have helped those around you to walk in freedom
You're beautiful inside and out, without a doubt
More gifts are springing forth from you
With eyes of love, He applauds you
For You have chosen to do His will
To love others as yourself and give your time
Even when it feels hard and you may want to unwind
"I see all that you sacrifice," He says
Thank you for loving my daughters well and helping resurrect areas in them that were dead."
You have led them into my freedom
Your mind is a deep well of wisdom
It springs forth like water in a time of need
So listen and heed the words of a wise mother
Her beauty shines!
Elegant and graceful
Full of character and integrity

He says, "your inheritance in me is a guarantee."
So lay it all down at my feet and see
How your cup overflows in me!

Titus 2:3 "Likewise, teach the older women to be reverent in the way they live, not to be slanderers or addicted to much wine, but to teach what is good." —ESV

Teachers of God

(A poem for those gifted with teaching the word of God)

You're a lover of His word
Without it, you'd go absurd
It is your daily food
That you always allude to
God is your rock, your fortress
And you never fail to lean on Him to feed your flock
You've been faithful to heed to His commands
And do whatever He demands
You're a laid-down lover
And you have not chosen any other
He is your source of life, your sustenance
Your heart has been expanded to love more deeply
As you freely open up your hands to Him
He unfolds His plans for you
Remember how much you grew
Who would've knew
That you would have a whole crew behind you
Let Him remind you
How much He's done
And He's only going to do more
As you implore your requests to Him
Watch how much He will show you
What He has in store.

Hebrews 13:17 "Obey your leaders and submit to them—
for they keep watch over your souls as those who will
give an account—so that they may do this with joy, not
groaning; for this would be unhelpful for you." —NIV.

Godly Fathers

(To godly fathers in the body of Christ with a pastoral heart)
A father figure to the masses
You're appointed and anointed
By you, children of the Kings inheritance are seeing their worth
You have won them over to the Lord
By showing them their value In His son
All the great things He has stirred in you, you have begun
And those you lead will do great exploits for our God
On this Earth, they will proclaim His name
They shall declare, "worthy is the Lamb who was slain."
To the nations abroad
You're rising up a generation that won't be a fraud
They will walk in authority
Because you've made living for Him and serving others your priority
Many were the frustrations in your early days
But God has shown you all of His faithful ways
Throughout all the testings, you have never failed to give Him glorious praise.
You ponder a lot in your head.
But He's always given you direction and has led you
He's never left you hanging by a thread
Walking with you, hand in hand
He has taught you how to walk into His plans
Even in your wilderness seasons
Remember how after all these years, He's changed your perception
To know His love for you as a good Father and deepen your affections
He is your source of protection

And the main one to always give you direction
So lean on Him for all your years
In you, He is always doing something brand new
"Faithful and True" is what He sings over you.

Titus:6-8 "Similarly, encourage the young men to be self-controlled. In everything set them an example by doing what is good. In your teaching, show integrity, seriousness and soundness of speech that cannot be condemned, so that those who oppose you may be ashamed because they have nothing bad to say about us.—ESV

To a Skilled Daughter

Quirky and fun
He loves to see you come alive in Him
Just be who you are!
In His sight, You shine bright like a star
"I have given you many dreams and visions."
He says, "Her life story I have written."
Her creativity is wrapped in her mind
Her God-given gifts are meant to shine
Lord, help her to see what you see
The time is now
The time is not "when or how."
Make it happen; allow
Trust in Him, and you will see
Seek heaven's door, and you will find
Your father has many different floors
Walk in and explore
All are yours
He longs to fill them up with more stories
Of you giving Him glory
He adores each unique thing about you
When you feel fear, heaven goes in an uproar, my dear
So my sister seek and ye shall find
I love you a lot; you're a dime
Knock, and the door shall be open to you
Use your gifts, take your steps of faith
Open Gods gate
He wants to give you so much more
Then, what you can imagine
If you only knew what He has in store
You'll never know till you fully try

You'll never know what fully lies
So wake up now
Because with God, it's all a beautiful surprise.

Matthew 7:7 "Keep on asking, and you will receive what you ask for. Keep on seeking, and you will find. Keep on knocking, and the door will be opened to you." —NLT.

Not My Own

My life is not my own
My home is not this place alone
I'm passing by
Restore me, Lord
Conformed to your image
The pattern of your likeness
I want to be like you
Love like you
Talk like you
Walk like you
Don't stop renewing my spirit till I'm more like you
Every day, don't let me go astray
Rid me of all the pride
Fill me up
What am I?
I don't want the world isn't inside of me
With your spirit, refresh me
I can't do this on my own
My flesh is weak
Your strength is everything
The reflection of your love is what I want to show them
Through my eyes
With each embrace and through my face
Let them see your light that shines so bright
For your glory, not mine
You get all the honor
I just love to glorify you, my Father
What does it mean to lay my life down fully?
Show me that life isn't about worldly crowns
Living by faith and not by what I'm seeing
Oh, to fully live
For you and others

Show me true sacrifice
What it means to pay the full price
For your kingdom and the sake of others
To love them as I love myself
Hidden in Christ so He can be revealed.

James 4:4 "You adulterous people, don't you know that friendship with the world means enmity against God? Therefore, anyone who chooses to be a friend of the world becomes an enemy of God." —NIV

Matthew 5:16 "Let your light so shine before men, that they may see your good works, and glorify your Father which is in heaven." —KJV

The Journey

Let His light shine on you
And when you're feeling blue
He's the one that you can run to
He's got your back
From every attack
Preserve you from the evil one; He will
And He shall fulfill
Every lack
Hearts stitching into one
Father spirit and son
A good work; He has begun
You and I into eternity
No more anguish or uncertainty
Enamored for Him
Removing the doubts within
I love you, Lord; you've shown me what is real
Oh, this love for you I feel
I walk on the water
I am your daughter
Not looking to the storm
The waves have ceased
Raves of your greatness, I beseech
Where is oh storm your norm over my life?
God has lifted my feet to greet the hurting and lost
An overcomer I am as I pick up my cross
Being led by your spirit
So the dying world can be fed with the truth
In my youth, I am vigorous and strong
Faithful like Ruth
You empower me to move on
I'm your favorite one, your song

God, I journey for you
Hold my hand and walk with me
Together forever, we shall be.

Psalm 119:19 "I am a stranger on earth; do not hide your commands from me. —NIV

First Love

I want to be left alone
Not answering as they blow up my phone
What is life?
I'm consumed with what could or can be
I like to be on my own, but I hate it too
Sitting alone in my room
Thinking of you and all the plans we made
We were supposed to go places, see faces
Change the world together
Sentimental
Now the years have gone by
Time flies
Have all these minutes been wasted?
As I get older, I start debating
Which direction I should take
I don't want to doubt my faith
Sometimes I feel like a fake
God save me from this heartbreak
There's only so much a sensitive girl like me can take
You said you won't let me be tested beyond what I can
bear
Days where I feel so low for no reason at all
You don't know what's making you unhappy, and it feels
hard to get out of bed.
Want to stay in instead
Life feels so hard
You wish the emptiness inside wouldn't be bringing you
into this downward spiral.
Your mind is paralyzed, and your purpose feels void
I lie awake most nights despising death
Wishing I could feel your breath
Once again, I can't even pretend I want this pain to end

Sometimes I can't comprehend why you had to go
So young and innocent
Pure and kind
There was none like you
Soft-spoken and gentle
We had plans to be together
You were special
Since your death, It's been hard for me to stay sane
I keep pursuers at arm's length
Don't let them get too deep
Oh, how much I weep over you
Some nights it's so hard to sleep
I'm weak.

I Trust

Though I'm surrounded by many, I feel lonely
Hopelessness screams at me
When will I enter into your promised land?
Running in circles for too long and the fear of man
Did my laps around the mountain
Make the paths straight already and lead me to your fountain
May I drink from it forevermore, and my spirit be lifted upright
My heart is heavy, and I don't feel right
Oh God, with arms raised high, I surrender
You will vindicate me
My judge and my deliverer
I can't count on my own strength
See my tears?
See my anguish?
You are big
Yet you still care
I know you're there
Closer to me than the air you are
Why do I worry?
When you know what I need
Why am I in a hurry?
When it's my heart, you heed to
I trust, I trust
You remember that I'm dust
You're my hope
I lay my head on the ground
And while the enemy lurks at me
I can rest while you work in me
You fight on my behalf
I can laugh

The battle is not my own
The Lord also laughs while He sits on His throne
Like Father like daughter
I can raise a hallelujah with a shout of praise! Yeah!
I will fix my gaze on my maker!
With outstanding joy, my Fathers shield encamps around me
You deploy your angels to protect on the left and right
This is my birthright
Covered by the blood of Jesus, the beauty of His sight
I love you, my God
Let all the earth praise Yahweh!

Hebrews 11:39 "These were all commended for their faith, yet none of them received what had been promised, since God had planned something better for us so that only together with us would they be made perfect." —NIV.

Matthew 6:33-34 "But seek first his kingdom and his righteousness, and all these things will be given to you as well. Therefore do not worry about tomorrow, for tomorrow will worry about itself. Each day has enough trouble of its own." —NIV

Psalm 2:4 "The One enthroned in heaven laughs; the Lord scoffs at them." —NIV

Isolation to Restoration

Sometimes I want to stay alone at home.
There are seasons when I don't want to be around anyone
Just my king
But here's the thing
I realize when we isolate ourselves for too long
The enemy makes us think that there is nothing wrong
He tricks us into thinking our flesh is strong
Like we can do it on our own
But my friends, we belong in God's home
We all belong to God and community
He commands us to live in full unity
If the apostles needed each other, then so do we
I've had many days where I wanted to make it on my own
So I tell you, you're not alone in your feelings
I understand; you want to find meaning
Some seasons feel so dry and wry
And you don't even want to try
And your soul can't find reasons to reach out
Being filled with so much doubt
You're tired of serving
And maybe just too hurt and disappointed
But I need to tell you something
You are what you declare
I know It's hard to hear when you feel like you can hardly
bear to hold on
To wait on for so long what you believed God had in store
for you
But through the testings, remember what He bore for you
And after the wrestling comes the blessing
And you are not your own
His sacrifice was enough
Oh beloved

Just look to the cross
Though humanity was at a loss
You were once too!
But He came, swept in, and made you brand new!
This is the hope and joy of your salvation!
God has saved you and has given you restoration
You can because of that man Christ Jesus
Meditate on the cross
Then you will begin to appreciate the cost
Rise up from your bed, you who feel dead
He is worthy of it all
His blood is enough
You who are called by your Father
Don't listen to that bluff of the enemy
Only Jesus can offer you full serenity
In Him alone is your God-given identity.

Genesis 32:26 "Then the man said, "Let me go, for it is daybreak." But Jacob replied, "I will not let you go unless you bless me." —NIV

One Thing

Listen
Come near
Let me tell you what Jesus did for me
I must testify now, you see
There have been challenging moments in my walk
But I won't disregard
All of the pruning the Lord has done in me
So many tears
So many fears
But He's held my hand through all my pilgrim years
His mercies every morning, give me a fresh start
I can never depart from my dazzling beloved
Where else can I go?
His love is the best I know
I'm learning how to love others and be an overflow
Of His reflection and radiance
Receiving His patience
A carrier of His presence and having Him be the essence
leading me is what I see.
Oh, how my heart is discerning His rhythm
And how I'm yearning to look more like Him
To lean in and feel what He says
And not be led by the voices of dread in my head
One thing I do desire
Is to seek His beauty
That my heart should always be ablaze for Him
And to never stop focusing my gaze on Him
And guess what
I'm not quitting So I win!

Psalm 27:4 "One thing I ask from the Lord, this only do I seek: that I may dwell in the house of the Lord all the days of my life,
to gaze on the beauty of the Lord and to seek him in his temple." —NIV

Worthy Lamb

His love has fulfilled me
Set me free from death
Where is your sting o death?
I eagerly await for Him
His face is what I long to see
My majesty, with His crown
In Him, I'm forever found
Take me to the cross, Lord
Everything else I count is lost
Every knee will bow
And every tongue shall confess your name
Now you sit at the Father's right hand
Let the cherubim around you sing,
"Holy, Holy, Holy, is the Lord God Almighty, who was who
is, and who is to come."
The whole earth is filled with His glory."
You're the lamb that was slain
Your death was not in vain
And every knee shall bow
And every tongue shall proclaim your holy name.

1 Corinthians 15:55-57 "Where, O death, is your victory?
Where, O death, is your sting?" The sting of death is sin,
and the power of sin is the law. But thanks be to God! He
gives us the victory through our Lord Jesus Christ. —NIV

Philippians 2:10-11 " that at the name of Jesus every knee
should bow, of those in heaven, and of those on earth, and
of those under the earth, and that every tongue should

confess that Jesus Christ is Lord, to the glory of God the Father." —NKJV

Revelation 4:8 "Each of these living beings had six wings, and their wings were covered all over with eyes, inside and out. Day after day and night after night they keep on saying, "Holy, holy, holy is the Lord God, the Almighty— the one who always was, who is, and who is still to come." —NLT.

Awaken

As I draw closer to the Spirit
He draws closer to me
His fire is in my being
It burns away all that I'm seeing
I can't hold in His words
I'm weary if I try
I'd rather die
There's no one else that satisfies
My beloved has me memorized
I see him when I look up into the skies
Oh, how my heart used to be paralyzed
Then He put a spark inside
He gave me the meaning of life
Oh, how great is your love for me!
Please take me back!
From before you formed me
And knew me
Before the womb
You who cause me to bloom
Where my story was written
In your book of life
Before you sent me out in the flesh
I want to know you
The three in one
Like how I used to
I want to be up there with you
Some things we will never know in this life
Oh, the mysteries of Christ.

Jeremiah 20:9 "But if I say, "I will not mention his word or speak anymore in his name," his word is in my heart like a fire, a fire shut up in my bones. I am weary of holding it in; indeed, I cannot." —NIV

Jeremiah 1:5 "I knew you before I formed you in your mother's womb. Before you were born I set you apart and appointed you as my prophet to the nations." —NLT

Who is He?

Jesus, your goodness overtakes me
Your kindness and mercy never forsake me
You're the God who created me
Jesus
You're awesome in all of your ways
All the sons of men praise you for all of their days
Your glory displays over all the Earth
Who is this man Christ Jesus?
He is the desire of the nations
The king of kings and Lord of Lords
Gird your sword
You mighty one
And win our inward wars
Lion of Judah, you roar
And your mercies soar over us!

"Gird your sword on your side, you mighty one; clothe yourself with splendor and majesty." - Psalm 45:3 —NIV

"Surely goodness and mercy shall follow me all the days of my life, and I shall dwell in the house of the LORD forever." - Psalm 23:6 —ESV.

Living Words

I want your words
I want to hear them alone
What are you saying?
Your words are set in stone.
Even if I have to go at it alone
I will
Just make this heart your home
How can I give all the glory and honor to you?
You're closer than the skin on my bones
My soul is ablaze with passion for you
Lord, how great is your love for me?
You've seen the bad that I've done
The battle in my mind that rages against you every single day?
My God, you're gracious and compassionate
Loving and dear
You've resurrected the dead areas inside
No need to hide
I can now see others through the lens of your eyes
My heart has a new light
It beams through every area of darkness
There is no more fright in me
You have put a new fight in me
You're the victory that I see
Christ in me has set me free!

Jeremiah 15:16 "When your words came, I ate them; they were my joy and my heart's delight, for I bear your name, LORD God Almighty." —NIV

Forgiven

You have stirred in me to trust in you.
I hear you saying, "forgive yourself, as I have forgiven you
The enemies accusations are weak
I am greater than he who is in the world
Hear now the words that I speak
You're redeemed and free
The enemy has schemed your thoughts
That burden isn't yours to carry, daughter
Allow my grace to fill you
You're holding on to your sin
Why are you wrestling with me?
And wrestling within?
Let go and surrender.
Allow me to take you out of this place of bondage
I have so much more in store for you
It can't be shown unless you allow me to heal that area
You can't walk out all that I have for you if you don't let
the truth of my forgiveness and word to be in your heart
Then you will start to be fully victorious
I know it's in your head
But instead, it has to be more than knowledge
You're trembling and crying
It's okay
Because you're willing
I know it feels hard
But you're finally fully letting go".

1 John 4:4 "You are from God, little children, and have
overcome them; because greater is He who is in you than
he who is in the world." —NASB

Have Mercy

God isn't going to use me in my perfect state
But when I'm broken so that I can relate
Sinners, free your mind of hate
Take His word
Sit down and meditate on the living God
Appreciate what He's done
Oh the Son, how He's won!
Oh Jesus, how My heart aches
For all the chains in the world that need to break
For your name's sake, God
Spare them
For mercy triumphs over judgment
God, you've seen our misery
The distress of injustice
Won't you stretch your arm once more?
Lord our God, with humble hearts, may we seek you while you are to be found
Have mercy on us, oh God Please have mercy on us! Could you help us?
Broken and contrite
Oh, forgive me, my God
And the sins of my nation
The blood spilled
The pride of unrepentance
Be gracious God
Remember our weak state
We need your spirit, oh God
The Life-Giver
Tear and rip the veil
Open our eyes so that we may see you rightly, Jesus
Rid these stony hearts
And give us hearts of flesh

Do a thing in our day, God
Help me to believe during my pilgrim days
That you will do a mighty work, God
May my eyes see the reviving work of the Lord
Dry bones coming to life
And souls being set free
By the power and name of Jesus Christ
Oh Lord, may your glory be magnified
What no eye has seen
And what no ear has heard
Lord, you're faithful to deliver your mighty word.

"Have mercy on me, O God, because of your unfailing love. Because of your great compassion, blot out the stain of my sins. Wash me clean from my guilt.
Purify me from my sin. For I recognize my rebellion; it haunts me day and night."
Psalm 51:1-3 —NLT

2 Chronicles 7:14 "and My people who are called by My name humble themselves, and pray and seek My face, and turn from their wicked ways, then I will hear from heaven, and I will forgive their sin and will heal their land." —NASB 1995

Habakkuk 1:5 "The LORD replied, "Look around at the nations; look and be amazed! For I am doing something in your own day, something you wouldn't believe even if someone told you about it." —NLT

Cloud 9

I'm on cloud 9 with you, Lord
I could scream it loud from the rooftops
Met Jesus, and every time I look at Him, my heart drops
I tell you my all, and you listen
I always want to be honest with you
The color of His eyes and the hurts of my past makes my savior cry
Jesus, I can't even lie; when I'm with you, I feel like I don't even need to try
You make my soul want to fly
You make me come so alive
Feeling so satisfied when I'm with you
It just gets better
I'm learning how to drown out the world
I want to be in this moment forever
Promise to be with me until I'm old, till beyond the boundaries of time
You're pouring out new wine
I don't care what people say; no one else makes me feel this way
I want the world to see
How amazing you are to me
They can say I'm insane
But like a magnet, I'm stuck to you and everything you do
Hand in hand, we're ready to go to the steeple
Awaiting the marriage supper
This is the beginning of the sequel
You'll destroy anything that gets in our way
You leave those forces of evil in dismay.

2 Corinthians 11:2 "I am jealous for you with a godly jealousy. I promised you to one husband, to Christ, so that I might present you as a pure virgin to him." —NIV.

Hosanna

Hosanna!
Hosanna in the highest
Blessed is He who comes in the name of The Lord!
Blessed is the sandaled feet of one who brings good news
The Lord brings good news
He reigns from heaven
He pours down His blessings on His children
The Lord smiles on those who practice His commands
Unto the righteous, He opens the floodgates of heaven
Blessed are the children of God!! All who serve Him faithfully.

Luke 19:38 "Blessings on the King who comes in the name of the Lord!
Peace in heaven, and glory in highest heaven!" —NLT

Printed in the United States
by Baker & Taylor Publisher Services